THE Achievers

Focus Personal & People Skills for Total Success

Empowers you for Fast-Track Success and Flow of Abundance & Good Luck

• Career • Business • Home • Family • Leadership

Anyone can Excell

Experience a new intensity & thrill to outperform yourself

G.P.S. Bawa

Second Edition

THE ACHIEVERS

First Edition: June 2001
Second Edition: 2005

No part of this book may be reproduced,
stored in a retrieval system or transmitted, in any form or by
any means, mechanical, photocopying, recording or otherwise,
without any prior written permission of the author.

© Copyright with the author

Price: Rs. 99.00

Published by Kuldeep Jain for

LEADS PRESS
an imprint of
B. Jain Publishers (P) Ltd.
1921, Street No. 10, Chuna Mandi,
Paharganj, New Delhi 110 055 (INDIA)
Phones: 2358 0800, 2358 1100, 2358 1300
Fax: 011-2358 0471; Email: bjain@vsnl.com
Website: **www.bjainbooks.com**

Printed in India by
J.J. Offset Printers
522, FIE, Patpar Ganj, Delhi - 110 092
Phones: 2216 9633, 2215 6128

ISBN: 81-8056-141-0
BOOK CODE: BB-5510

ABOUT THE AUTHOR

The Book is the product of the collective wisdom of management gurus, author's personal experiences and observations in life and specialisation in Public Relations.

G.P.S. Bawa is M.A. English from Punjab University and M.A. Public Relations from The American University (Washington D.C.). A former diplomat, he held diplomatic assignments in media relations in Bhutan, U.K., USA, Canada and the erstwhile Soviet Union. He was also Editor of the World Press Review for 3 years.

He has been engaged in taking up motivational lectures, seminars on communications, and looking after media relations of international events. He has authored five books, the most commented upon being : Economic and Technical Cooperation among Developing Countries. He has contributed a number of papers in learned journals and published dozens of feature articles in newspapers.

CONTENTS

PART-I – INTERPERSONAL SKILLS

1. THE CONCEPT TAP — 3
2. SUCCESS IS A NATURAL PROCESS — 9
3. SIGNIFICANCE OF ATTITUDES — 13
   a. Attitudes can be altered — 15
   b. How to develop positive attitudes — 16
   c. Negative attitudes lead to failure — 20
   d. How to tap power of positive attitudes — 20
   e. What makes a person successful — 24
4. SELF – INDOCTRINATION — 29
5. HOW TO OVERCOME FAILURE — 33
   a. What leads to failure — 33
   b. Strategy to overcome failure — 42
6. MOTIVATION BEGINS WITH YOU — 47
   a. What motivates employees — 49
   b. New motivation strategies — 52
   c. Techniques for motivation — 53
7. VISION — 55
   a. Reasons for lack of Vision — 56
   b. Handicaps and problems — 57
   c. How to realise your Vision — 58
8. BOOST YOUR WILLPOWER — 61
9. GOALS — 65
   a. Goals – The highway to Top Achievement — 65
   b. Steps for setting Goals — 66

	c.	The Purpose Goal	68
	d.	Value of Goals	70
10.		DEVELOPING CORE COMPETENCIES	75
11.		TIME MANAGEMENT	81
12.		MANAGING STRESS	85

PART-II – INTERACTIVE SKILLS

1.		RELATIONSHIPS	97
2.		NETWORKING AND INTERNET	105
	a.	Social and Professional Networking	105
	b.	Inter-Business Networking	108
	c.	Global Corporate Networking	108
	d.	Internet - Impact of, and Approach to	110
3.		SYNERGY	115
4.		COMMUNICATION SKILLS	121
	a.	Barriers and Distortion	122
	b.	Effective Communication	123
	c.	Basic Personal Communication	125
	d.	How to get Favourable Response	128
	e.	Steps to Win Over Customer	130
	f.	Skills for Handling Small Group Communication	131
	g.	Improving Internal Communications	134
5.		COMMUNICATION AND SUCCESSFUL JOB	137
6.		YOU CAN GET THE JOB YOU WANT	140
7.		LEADERSHIP	145
	a.	Leadership Development	146
	b.	Identifying High Performers	148
	c.	Effective Leadership Strategies	149
	d.	Leadership Styles	149
	e.	Leadership and Public Speaking	154
8.		CELEBRATE LIFE	157

WHY THIS BOOK ?

This book offers you a new concept in personality development. It is an attempt to restore the focus of personality development to nurturing of the individual into Top Achieving People (TAP).

The book has been specially written for people like you and me – students in schools and colleges, managers, executives and housewives. It creates an awareness in you of the purpose of your life and leads you to develop the capacity and potential to dazzle the destiny by working towards higher level of commitment.

There has been a paradigm shift in thinking and perceptions of the people in the new Information Technology environment. People today are more competitive and ambitious. They think in terms of achieving excellence in life. In tune with the high aspirations of the young people and to keep them continuously focused, the discussion on GOALS has been supplemented to include the process of planning for the grand goal or the purpose of life. This would meet the high expectations of the Top Achieving People (TAP).

High expectations are the key to everything.

...SAM WALTON

This book offers a sort of construction manual. It describes all the tools that you need. It opens up new avenues of thinking and offers a blueprint. It takes you step by step through this exciting journey to your GOAL.

It helps you to organise yourself from within by developing synergy of your three fundamental positive energies viz. (1) Intention with Awareness, (2) Attributes and Skills, and (3) Core Competencies. This concentration of three energies propels you to the achievement of your highest goal.

The book adds a new dimension to your potential by showing you how networking and internet can be used as additional effective tools.

In the next two decades we are going to need very huge inputs of TAP manpower in all spheres of human activity to sustain the tempo of development and to "deliver" the country.

While individual efforts will always be there, we need a coordinated and well planned governmental and corporate sector action towards formulating the new education policy and investment in education for the creation of intellectual capital. These people, according to TAP concept, will be totally self-integrated individuals.

The higher the quality and the competency levels of the knowledge capital, the better will be the country's ability to withstand global competition and the onslaught of technological and market changes. These people will power the country to be a major player in the new socio-economic environment.

G.P.S. Bawa
New Delhi.

PART-I

INTERPERSONAL SKILLS

THE CONCEPT-TAP

*An invasion of armies can be resisted,
but not an idea whose time has come.*

...**Victor Hugo**

Top Achieving People (TAP) concept is a natural and spontaneous outcome of the current highly competitive environment. It is in keeping with the high aspirations and ambitions of the young people. The new Information Technology environment has raised their expectations. They think in terms of attaining excellence and high achievement.

The world is continuously shrinking in terms of distance and space. Competition is rising, threatening to overtake the mediocre or the tired professionals. Young people are prepared to take on the new challenges. They aim to be the best, almost perfect.

TAP concept is tailor-made for these young achievers. It helps them channelise their abundant positive energies towards the fulfilment of their purpose in life through total self-integration. TAP helps them to develop into good human beings who make to the top not only in their chosen field but also shine in all spheres of human activity. These people have a highly developed team spirit. They are keen participants in social welfare activities and help others to achieve their goals. They have an enlightened and "inspired mind" primed to make a mark in life.

TAP individuals are thus organised from within and have a natural "intention" to make a mark in life. Excellence seeps into all areas of their character and personality and gives them more control over their emotions and state of mind.

> *All work happens through intention. You intend – I want to go somewhere – and you go. All life moves with intentions. If I don't have an intention to raise my hand, it will not raise... All work happens through intention*
>
> ...SRI SRI RAVI SHANKAR
> [THE ART OF LIVING]

All human action is the outcome of intention and it gets its direction through awareness. The TAP concept focuses on tapping your awareness of what you want to do with your life and your intention to get going.

According to Dr. Deepak Chopra, "Intention combined with detachment leads to life centered present moment awareness. And when action is performed in present moment awareness, it is most effective. Your intent is for the future, but your attention is on the present".

From the above we deduce the following formula :

Intention + Awareness = Effective Action

This awareness releases high level of mental and physical energies for action towards developing positive attributes, skills and core competencies. The three – phase energy thus generated goes on to develop synergy towards the final thrust to the goal. The following diagram very clearly illustrates the interaction and routes of these positive energies to the achievement of your life's purpose.

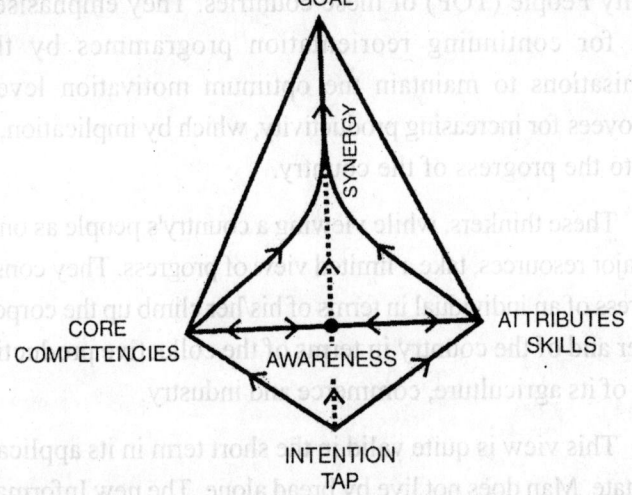

It is clear from the foregoing that TAP is an inclusive concept. A top achiever knows the value and power of synergy. He/she is aware that an achievement invariably includes others. So naturally in the process of the achievement, he helps others to realise their personal goals.

We cannot help ourselves without helping others

...**PROVERB**

Top Achieving People (TAP) have the right attitude blended with perfect aptitude. They are people just like you and me who have made extraordinary accomplishments as a result of their tremendous endeavours and strong determination and contributed to the progress of the country.

TAP FOR MASSES

Progress in democratic and industrial societies has come about through the total collective quality of the people of these countries. But some leading thinkers and management gurus view the progress in leading democratic societies and their industrial and business organisations as the outcome of inputs by Total Quality People (TQP) of these countries. They emphasise the need for continuing reorientation programmes by these organisations to maintain the optimum motivation level of employees for increasing productivity, which by implication, will lead to the progress of the country.

These thinkers, while viewing a country's people as one of its major resources, take a limited view of progress. They consider progress of an individual in terms of his/her climb up the corporate ladder and of the country in terms of the collective productivity level of its agriculture, commerce and industry.

This view is quite valid in the short term in its application to a state. Man does not live by bread alone. The new Information Technology environment in today's democratic societies and the rising aspirations of their people cannot be sustained only by the quality and efficiency of their managers at the productivity level but by developing Top Achieving People (TAP) at the masses level.

Democracy is based upon the conviction
that there are extraordinary possibilities
in ordinary people

...**HARRY EMERSON FOSDICK**

The sudden jump start in Information Technology has made us sit up. We are watching with wonder the fast changes in the way we live, communicate, work and play. Our emotions have been aptly described in the following lines of W. Wordsworth composed during the French Revolution :

> *Bliss it was in that dawn to be alive*
> *But to be young was very heaven*
>
> ...**W. WORDSWORTH**

In the current environment of excitement and expectancy, old concepts and way of thinking are falling by the way side. Mere aiming for success, "different goals" or targets is not the in thing. People's sights are raised and their aim is very high.

We have attempted here to build-up and channelise the positive enthusiasm of young people. A step by step approach has been described in the succeeding pages to develop their total potential for excellence. It enables them to integrate their attributes and skills to develop core competencies to make the final thrust to their goal in life and become Top Achieving People.

WHAT SUCCESS MEANS TO YOU

You have to define in your mind what success means to you before you start building bridges to get going. It was John Forster Dulles who said, "If you want to build castles in the air, go ahead and do it. But try to put foundations underneath."

Defining success is the first step towards achieving it.

PHILOSOPHY OF SUCCESS

> Work harder than any one else,
> work at something you enjoy
> and keep working... Every man
> should struggle to love
> what he does when he
> cannot do what he loves

PHILOSOPHY OF TAP

> Top Achievers begin where they
> are and with what they have

The only place success comes before work is in the dictionary

...Donald Kendall

SUCCESS IS A NATURAL PROCESS

The very fact you have laid your hands on this book YOU ARE A WINNER. You have taken charge of your life. You have a purpose to achieve. And success comes naturally to those who have an earnest desire for it.

All human beings are created in the image of God, say the holy books. Every man and woman is born with an in-built capacity for success.

There is no secret, no miracle, no special genius required for achieving success in life. Man wants to climb. He cannot resist the urge to move upwards, not only metaphorically but also physically.

A seed that is sown grows into a plant and bears flowers or fruit. Care has to be taken that the seed is healthy and weeding is done regularly. In the same way human beings are blessed with the natural instinct for achieving success in life.

Just as it is the nature of the sun to shine and the stars to sparkle, so is the human nature blessed to make the dream manifest in physical form.

You have only to be in harmony with nature. Observe and imbibe the natural laws of life that have come down to us through great thinkers, philosophers and religious teachers and apply these methodically and with dedication to achieve your goal in life.

It has been very aptly said :

Watch your thoughts, they become your action;
Watch your actions, they become your habits;
Watch your habits they become your character;
Watch your character, that is your ultimate destiny.

From the foregoing we deduce four eternal truths of life as follows :

1. Think no evil
2. Speak no evil
3. See no evil
4. Hear no evil

ETERNAL TRUTHS – PATH TO SUCCESS

'Dharma' emanates from the Prakrit word "Dhammo" which means "support". Anything that supports life positively is Dharma. All religious teachers and thinkers ask us to follow the eternal truths to light our path in the rough and tumble of our journey through life.

> *Fortitude, forgiveness rule*
> *over the mind*
> *Not taking other's goods*
> *against their will,*
> *Cleanliness, control over the*
> *senses too,*
> *Alert intelligence learning,*
> *and truthfulness,*
> *Not giving way to anger*
> *such are the*
> *Unfailing marks of the*
> *eternal Dharma*
>
> **...Manu Smriti**

You may naturally ask how religion or Eternal Truths derived from it can help achieve success when religion shuns "maya" i.e. material success. This has been beautifully answered by Sri Ramakrishna as follows :

> *Ornaments cannot be made of pure gold. Some alloy must be mixed with it. A man totally devoid of Maya will not survive more than twenty one days. So long as the man has a body, he must have some Maya – Maya however small it may be, to carry on the functions of the body.*
>
> ...**Sri Ramakrishna**

A study of biographies of great achievers reveals that they had a balanced approach towards religious piety and "maya". Buddha's Middle Way was very correctly interpreted and applied by them. For Middle Way is not a compromise but a better, High way of life.

Life is continually moving forward. It contains within itself infinite possibilities and unlimited capacity for self-development. It can rise above total obsession for maya or self-gratification. It is capable of vertical movement.

According to the scholar of Jainism, Acharya Mahaprajna, the wholeness of the life of a social being can be viewed in four dimensions : desire, money, religion and liberation. "A man living in these four dimensions lives holistically or has a balanced way of life. It is essential for him to develop his social consciousness alongwith his religious consciousness... That makes for a balanced life".

The philosophy of a balanced approach to life is most significant for young people in the new millennium. It makes for wholesome and total self-integration. It is only through balanced development in all fields that a social being can have self-fulfilment.

In the following chapters, we will breakdown the discussion into broad categories for greater clarity and focus, and analyse, deduce and chalk out a blueprint for achieving your dream and go on to synchronise your positive energies to become Top Achieving People (TAP).

SIGNIFICANCE OF ATTITUDES

Life is raw material. We are artisans. We can sculpt our existence into something beautiful, or debase it into ugliness; it is in our hands.

...**Cathy Better**

Our habits and thinking go to weave the fabric of our life. These together determine the way we think.

Habit means compulsive need, inclination or tendency; it reflects the prevailing character or quality. That's the reason it has been said that if you cut the first letter of 'habit', 'a bit' will remain. If you cut off the second letter 'bit' will still remain. If you cut off the third letter, 'it' will remain. So we have to be on guard against negative or bad habits for these influence our thinking.

The way we habitually look at and react to the goings on in life goes to form our attitude. Our habit-bound, pattern recognising emotive thinking determines the positive or negative quality of our attitude. We should adopt a positive or creative attitude towards life. This you cannot do in a day. It is a gradual process, but you must start right now. The one teaching which has been given to us by all the great teachers of humanity is that man is his own friend and his own foe. If you would be your own friend, adopt a positive attitude towards life.

What is it to have a positive attitude ? It is not that a man with positive attitude is not affected by negative happenings in life. Life is a criss - cross of light and shade, happiness and sorrow. It has its highs and lows, glory and setbacks. But a person with the positive attitude refuses to be overawed by negative influences and emotions; he/she does not dwell on the negative side of life. He tries to look for a bright chink in a so-called hopeless situation. It is this attitude to continue to expect good things in the worst of circumstances that carries a person through a difficult situation. "It is an inviolable law of life, that when you expect good, good will come to you," says J.P. Vaswani.

We are told of a classic story of a CEO of a large company, who seeing the drop in sale in certain territories called the sale representatives to a meeting. At this meeting he simply pasted a large piece of white paper on the wall and placed a black dot at the centre of this paper. He asked the representatives one by one what they saw on the paper. Everyone replied, "A black dot". When he had gone the round, he called them again and asked if they saw anything besides the black dot. They all answered in the negative. It is then that he told them : "This is your great tragedy. You only see the black dot. You don't see the white expansive space that surrounds the black dot. Now go back to your territories and stop seeing the black dot. Look out for opportunities instead of difficulties, and you will find that the sales of our products will go up."

Attitudes are the foundation of all activity in life. Correct or positive attitudes of the people make for progress of a country. A country's population is one of its major resources. Positive attitudes of its people produce fast progress in its agriculture, industry and social institutions and, in short, in all spheres of human activity. The majority of the population of highly developed countries have positive attitudes. The people are purposeful and goal oriented.

The importance of positive attitudes has made social institutions and business organisations to pay more attention towards education and training of the individual. Business and industry consider training the managers and workers for developing positive attitudes and skills as an integral part of human resource development.

Management gurus describe such purposeful and goal oriented people as Total Quality People (TQP) and emphasise that all organisations must fund training programmes for the development of TQP workers for all-round progress.

ATTITUDES CAN BE ALTERED

Our attitudes are formed during our childhood. These are influenced by our environment, our experiences during the formative years and our education. We have positive attitude if we had exposure to positive influences. Negative attitude is the outcome of negative influences. It can, however, be changed with great persistence and willpower.

Our attitude plays a significant role in determining whether any activity (our daily work) is pleasant or not. It affects our productivity as well as the quality of our output. Now if you have a natural positive attitude you have no problem. Otherwise whenever you get up in the morning you repeat three times to yourself : "I like my work and am proud of my workmanship". You will find a positive change taking place in your attitude. If you keep on repeating this exercise day after day and consciously keep this in view during the day, your persistence and willpower will permanently alter your attitude to the positive.

Positive attitude is the mother of luck. Look at any successful person, you will find positive attitude a dominant trait of his/her character. This characteristic is totally within our control. We are responsible for the way we look at life. Our positive attitude is the first step towards success.

An infinite potential lies locked within us. We are unaware of it because we think of ourselves as limited, restricted creatures. There can be no limit to what we can do and achieve. It is said that whatever the mind of man imagines, human ingenuity puts it into reality. Of course it needs patience, persistence and hard work.

HOW TO DEVELOP POSITIVE ATTITUDES

Every journey begins with the first step and progresses stage by stage. Having a positive attitude is the first step towards success. It provides us with positive energy to accomplish our goal in life. Achievers distinguish themselves by having positive attitudes.

We make our own roads; each one of us. It is entirely up to us whether we travel freely and joyously or miserable and overawed by sorrows. Even if the road itself is non-existent, we can ensure that the road is formed for us to walk on it with the power of positive attitudes.

We will now discuss guidelines on what positive attitudes are and how we develop these :

OPTIMISM

Some people are born optimist. Optimism is an inborn trait in them. But in most cases, it is an acquired or a carefully cultivated habit. There are others who are pessimists. They see only the dark and the negative side of things. This has been beautifully described by Fredrick Langbridge. Two men look out through the same bars : one sees the mud, and one the stars".

Coming out of a church one Sunday morning, William Dean Howells and Mark Twain were caught in heavy rain. "Do you think it will stop ?" asked Howells. "It always has," replied Twain.

Optimism nurtures and boosts hope and confidence and our will to survive in the most difficult of circumstances and in dire adversity. It helps us to count our blessings and encourages us to go on.

Let's then be up and doing
With a heart for any fate
Still achieving still pursuing
Learn to labour and to wait

...**W. H. Longfellow**

There is no need to be downcast if things do not work out our way. No failure is final. King Robert Bruce, after his crushing defeat, lay on his couch in pensive mood. He watched an injured spider repeatedly climbing up a wall and falling down. He saw it finally climbing up the wall in the seventh attempt.

You know what – King Bruce defeated his enemy in the next engagement.

PATIENCE AND HOPE

Positive thinking or attitude aids your patience, increases your positive energy and gives you hope "to look for other doors that are wide open." You may trip but you get up and go on to think of attaining your goal through following a different approach.

DO NOT ANTICIPATE TROUBLE

If you adopt positive thinking, you will be able to resist the habit to anticipate trouble and to worry about what may never happen. We know of certain people who make themselves prisoners of their imagination which totally incapacitates them. It was Benjamin Franklin who said : "Do not anticipate trouble, or worry about what may never happen, keep in the sunlight." Achievers, instead of worrying about future, prepare for it and make it a bright one.

CULTIVATE FAITH

Faith can move mountains, they say. Firmly believe in your infinite capacity to overcome obstacles in your path. Everyone of us have faced so called insurmountable problems in our lives. One thing that helps through all these is faith. Faith in our ability, faith in the goodness of the world, faith in our friends and relations, in short faith in all its manifestations.

Faith is seeing with the eyes of your heart, says Dada J.P. Vaswani a scientist turned saint. Just as with our physical eyes, we see with the eyes of the heart. We get frustrated and defeated when the eyes of the heart are closed. When these eyes open we realise : "All that has happened has happened for the best, all that will happen will happen for the best. For God has a plan for everyone of us, and there is a purpose in every little thing that happens to us." Whittier, the great American poet said : "When faith is lost ...the man is dead!"

It also helps to spend a few minutes being grateful. It is an emotion not studied enough. When we feel gifted there is often a natural tendency to focus on the giver, and we want to give back.

Don't Carry Tension of One Moment to Another

Once the harsh words have been spoken – you have said sorry or the person has said so – just forget the whole episode. Before you take up another task, just pause and relax in the thought of unity of all life. This thought cleanses you and soothes internally and does not allow tension to build up. It enables you to keep up and build human relationships.

Practice Relaxation

The simplest way to relax is to sit cross legged or in a straight back chair and practice silence for five minutes in the morning and evening. Achievers find time in their busy schedules to relax and enjoy the beauty and bounty of nature. They cultivate a hobby to make themselves happy and relaxed.

Help Others

Be not merely good, be good for someone. One must try to experience the joy of helping others in need of kind words, friendly words or supporting words. We should show our concern for the people around us. The happiness that we give to others comes back to us. It is twice 'blest' like the quality of mercy.

Let us live our life like trees that provide shelter and fruit and not potted plants. Let us develop strong roots of great ambitions and strong will out of which grows the trunk, leaves and everything that we aspire for. The results that we obtain will be the fruits of our actions. Let us live as big tree type who help others.

NEGATIVE ATTITUDES LEAD TO FAILURE

> *The mind is its own place*
> *and in itself*
> *Can make a heaven of hell*
> *and a hell of heaven*
>
> ...JOHN MILTON

We shall attempt here to briefly outline how negative attitudes have negative effect on our personality and, if not checked or corrected, make us a total failure :

- Success lies in the mind. What you think about your own ability, often leads to either success or failure.
- Negative thinking is equal to failure.
- It distorts our perception of an issue or event and clouds our judgement.
- It is contagious and should be avoided as you would a highly infectious disease.
- Negative attitude blows everything out of perspective. Problems appear to be daunting and insurmountable.
- Negative attitude takes the joy out of life by reducing hope. It causes depression and saps our positive energy.
- It freezes our willpower. We are neither able to make use of our potential nor attempt to put up our best effort. Any half-hearted attempt is bound to be a failure.

HOW TO TAP POWER OF POSITIVE ATTITUDES

Our positive attitudes and patterns of behaviour are our resources through which we can build up strength to face the goings on in life. We could draw on their energy and respond to the varied difficult situations and resolve these effectively.

We can all train ourselves to be incorrigibly positive thinking people. This attitude can be acquired by anyone. And I mean everyone.

We are all product of our own thinking. The trigger to the "will to act" is the product of what happens in those billions of brain cells. We have to stimulate this will to act with our desire or intention.

A few guidelines or principles that follow will help you improve your ability to tap the vital energy of positive thinking :

DO IT NOW

A thousand mile journey begins with a single step. Take the step and see the miles melt away under your feet, Do it now. Do not postpone anything or any job. Just Do it. This will help you live in the present and build-up a positive attitude. It will give you energy and fulfilment. This positive energy will automatically prepare you for a better future by building your positive self-esteem and insulating you from negative people and habits.

*You can't build a reputation on
what you are going to do*

...HENRY FORD

VISUALISE YOURSELF AS SUCCESSFUL PERSON

Top Achieving People in any field use mental imaging. Research shows mental practice can have the same effect as real practice. Psychologist Gerald Epstein says. "In many ways, the brain doesn't know the difference between an actual and an imagined event. By creating mental images for success you are, in fact, creating memories. You are creating a new model of behaviour."

What is man if he does not have a dream to live for. The beauty of the dream will lead him on. What you imagine today determines what you will be tomorrow.

DEVELOP CONFIDENCE AND PURPOSE

To develop confidence and stronger purpose in your life you have to neutralise the mind of fear. Feed your sub-conscious mind with words of positive planning, persistence, enthusiasm and faith. You have to indoctrinate yourself with the message of achievement. You have to dream your little dream and then accomplish it piece by piece.

Your strength becomes the strength of ten – because you believe in yourself. Believe and achieve. Such is the law of success. Plan every day to do something you think you cannot do. That is the way to develop strength, courage and confidence.

BE COURTEOUS AND PAY ATTENTION

Despite the fast pace of life you can get work done, make friends and leave an impression of your personality on others simply by showing courtesy and paying full attention. This positive attitude will add value to human interactions and make for goodwill, harmony and peace.

SHOW APPRECIATION, MAKE THEM FEEL IMPORTANT

Prompt and gracious recognition of an individual or an employee's good deed or good work can serve as a positive reinforcement. If you fulfil this need in others, you get appreciation and attention in return.

Catch them doing something RIGHT is fast becoming the 'mantra' of progressive bosses in business and industry.

LOOK FOR THE BEST IN EVERYONE

The attitude to look for the best in everyone makes others

feel good about themselves. They try their best to come up to your expectation, and you secure their fullest cooperation. It creates a harmonious productive environment.

We should make a conscious effort to appreciate, encourage and love our fellow-men and women to draw out the best in them.

Look Out For Great New Ideas

Positive thinkers are always quick to grasp the best new ideas. Great new ideas create human interest, generate power and increase achievers potential for success. The human mind is creative. Let it create new thoughts. If you cling to old thoughts and keep repeating them, you will not grow in wisdom. Look for and create new ideas and experiment with these.

> *It is a lesson which all history teaches wise men,*
> *to put trust in ideas, and not in circumstances*
>
> ...R. Waldo Emerson

Be Generous – Avoid Pettiness

Positive thinkers do not waste time and energy in discussing petty and insignificant things. They do not attach any importance to petty things as these can sometime create reactions that are outrageous. For instance, we are reminded of the story of a Chinese emperor who once went to war over the breaking of a teapot.

Deepak Chopra in his book, The Seven Spiritual Laws of Success, says that most people spend ninety per cent of their time defending their points of view, wasting energy and nurturing resentment and hurtfulness. He adds that if we give up this habit, refusing to get into arguments, then we gain access to creative energy that can be gainfully used.

DEVELOP SPIRIT OF SERVICE

People with positive attitudes have a natural instinct for service before self. This strengthens their moral fibre and makes them more dynamic, forceful and worthy of respect. Such people are hard to resist. They are doers and easily get the cooperation of others in accomplishing projects of human welfare. There is every reason people should cooperate with someone who is trying to help them. These people contribute to all-round goodness and make this world a better place.

WHAT MAKES A PERSON SUCCESSFUL

*Big shots are only little shots
that keep on shooting*

...**Christopher Morley**

How you start is important, but it is how you finish that counts. In the race for success, speed is less important than stamina. The sticker outlasts the sprinter.

...**Forbes**

An achiever has a burning desire to accomplish a chosen and worthy goal. This desire for success pervades his/her whole being and can find relief or resolution only on its realisation. It is this most powerful feeling that drives him/her to achieve success in life.

Asked about secret of success, Socrates counter questioned the youngman what he would want the most if he were drowning. The boy replied, "Air". Socrates told him, well, that was the secret of success. If you desired something as you would the air, then you surely get it.

COMMITMENT

Commitment provides the winning edge in any situation. The difference between the best and the worst sports team is in their emotional responses. The winning team has commitment and they make the extra effort. A person with commitment enjoys tougher competition. It provides him/her greater incentive and motivation to give the best performance.

The tougher the challenge, the greater is the development of one's potential. People who play to win thrive on pressure.

RESPONSIBILITY

Responsibility means not blaming anyone or anything for our situation, including ourselves. One can have a creative response to the situation. Again a duty which is visualised by a person as a desire becomes a delight says George Gritter. Men of character never shirk from their responsibility. They evaluate all aspects before taking the most appropriate decision or action. If the decision or action turns out to be wrong, they have the courage to accept responsibility and learn from the error in judgement.

HARD WORK

Nothing has ever been achieved without hard work. As a matter of fact, it is common knowledge that genius is three-fourth hard work and one-fourth intelligence. The harder you work, the luckier you get, says Henry Ford.

The average person puts only 25% of his energy and ability into his work. The world takes off its hat to those who put in more than 50% of their capacity, and stands on its head for those few and far between souls who devote 100%.

...ANDREW CARNEGIE

CHARACTER

Character is like a tree and reputation like its shadow

...ABRAHAM LINCOLN

Character refers to sum total of the characteristics - values, beliefs and personality - possessed by a person.

It is said character building starts from the womb and continues right till the tomb. We do not get it ready made on our lap like Newton's apple. We create, mould and build ourselves into the kind of person we want to be. "Character does not need success; it is success", says Shiv Khera.

DELIVER MORE THAN YOU PROMISE

To get ahead of your competition and to make an impact, you should be always ready to deliver more than you are paid for or expected to. This provides you with the winning edge. You become more valuable. People start respecting you and readily follow your advice.

PERSISTENCE

Failures and setbacks are stepping stones to success in life. As a matter of fact most success stories have great failures in their background. Failures did not discourage these persons. Rather these acted as a driving force and made these people humble and more humane. While working on his electric bulb, Thomas Edison failed almost 10,000 times. He did not give up. Each time he bounced back from his failure with renewed energy and ultimately turned the stumbling blocks into stepping stones for success.

*If at first you don't succeed
Try, try, again. Try and Try again.*

...W. EDWARD HICKSON

CREATIVITY – AIM FOR EXCELLENCE

"Whatever your life's work is, do it well. A man should do his job so well that the living, the dead and the unborn could do it no better."

...MARTIN LUTHER KING, JR.

A successful person takes pride in his/her performance. He works hard and takes keen interest in his job and is satisfied only with the very best effort. Lord Tennyson kept on revising, editing and chiselling his poems till every stanza, every line and every word began to glitter like a real gem.

A thing of beauty is a joy for ever. People remember the excellence of effort in any sphere of activity. They seldom bother to remember how fast you did a job. A good performer derives satisfaction from the excellence of his effort and finds it rewarding in itself.

WE ARE CONTINUOUSLY LEARNING

Learning is a life-long process. A person who stops learning stops growing. The more curious we are, the more creative we become. The first principle of learning is to be humble and always ask someone knowledgable about what you do not know. This means you should find yourself a "guru", a guide to whom you can turn to when in doubt. The guide may not give you all the answers, but will show you the right direction. Now you may be climbing up a wrong wall; the guide will tell you simply to put the same ladder against the opposite wall to reach your goal.

PLANNING

Planning is the most important element that goes into success of any kind and in any field of endeavour. It is the hallmark of all achievers. Napoleon was once asked the reason for his withdrawal from a particular battle front. He replied it was a part of the war strategy. He always planned to win the war and cared not if he lost a few battles in the process.

Planning is 100 per cent preparation, practice and hard work. And this makes the difference between being a winner or a loser.

A planned effort is already half done. Your direction is clear. You know all that is required of you and are all set to attain your chosen goal.

COMMON SENSE GUIDE TO SUCCESS

AIM TO WIN ALWAYS

- Learn from your competition.
- Learn from other's mistakes.
- Seek company of people of integrity.
- Deliver more than you promise.
- Success does not fall on your lap. You work for it.
- Build on your strengths.
- Have a long range view.
- Make your decisions after mastering details.
- Honesty is the best policy.
- Don't let up. Keep going until you are finished.
- When all else fails, lower your standards.

SELF - INDOCTRINATION

TOP ACHIEVING PEOPLE THINK BIG

You can become a "self-making" man by thinking Big. It is the rule of success that if you think big, and are organised to go after your goal, you will succeed. Why not repeat to yourself the words that will get you there ? Why not indoctrinate those words of success into yourself every day ?

In indoctrinating yourself for bigger and better achievements, there is no place in your vocabulary for self pity, according to Frank James of Motivational Institute. There is no place for sympathy or fear either.

In order to free the mind of fear, discouragement and doubt, you have to feed your subconscious mind with words of positive planning, enthusiasm, determination and faith. You have to indoctrinate yourself with the message of achievement.

HOW TO SELF-INDOCTRINATE YOURSELF

We are all controlled by suggestions from day to day. These are used to help release positive mental energy to build up our potential, abilities and talents. By a series of command control patterns, you can indoctrinate anything into your mind or minds of others that you desire. You fine tune yourself for success through self imposed ideas and suggestions.

Suggestion is a repeated and regular planting of a "purposeful and persuasive" success message. This is planted by the sub-conscious and conscious mind to lead you on to success.

Technique One

Repeat the success message to yourself with complete concentration daily before going to sleep and after waking up. French druggist psychologist Emile Coue persuaded people to start the day by repeating, "Day by day, in every way, I am getting better and better" twenty times. Those who tried it found the results to be amazing.

Silva, however, says that we should also programme our sub-conscious every day by repeating "Negative thoughts and negative suggestions have no influence over me and at any level of mind". He claims these self statements have far reaching impact on gearing you up for top performance.

Rev. Charles Shelton, Professor of Psychology, in his book, Achieving Moral Health : An Exercise Plan for Your Conscience, says by devoting a few minutes every day you can make your conscience shipshape. The first step is to have some "quality solitude" time. The quiet time is necessary to collect one's thoughts and emotions. "Just take the time and say, 'I am a person of conscience' 10 or 15 times a day. That simple act can start a revolution. It raises consciousness. It raises the oughtness and the word ought has a moral, compelling thrust to it." According to Shelton, the very action of saying you have a good conscience will prompt you to re-examine your actions. "In most of us there is this inarticulated or unspoken desire for goodness. What we need to do is to recognise it in ourselves", he concludes.

There is a common thread running through all the above suggestions of fixing a particular worthy idea in our subconscious by repeating the same at our conscious level. This sub-conscious knowledge in combination with our desire to cultivate the idea builds it up into a conscious positive attitude.

Technique Two

VISUALISE YOURSELF A WINNER : Achievers in many fields use mental imaging to serve as a mental rehearsal. We learn of several top surgeons who run a motion picture of the procedure of the operation the night before a complicated surgery or a new procedure. They even do a brainstorming session with other specialists to fill in the gap or to re-assure themselves. Mental imaging thus serves a most critical function in making them calm, collected and more confident to handle a new procedure.

Professional athletes also follow the same practice to enhance their performance. The visualisation process enables them to "imagine the building blocks and proceed step by step" to the desired purpose.

Psychologist Bernie Zibbergeld opines that imaging is no doubt helpful but "it is not a substitute for action but a supplement to it".

No doubt one has to be patient to achieve results. It requires considerable practice and effort.

Technique Three

The third technique is nothing but a common sense approach to organising yourself to develop a directional thrust for your positive actions. It is a combination technique comprising self-indoctrination at the conscious level and self-motivation.

In this method, you write the following on a card and concentrate on your positive forward thrust towards success.

1. **MY GOALS**
    a. .... Know your objective.
    b. .... Motivate yourself by
    c. .... writing it down.

d. ....
e. ....

2. **MY TALENTS**
   a. .... Write down your talents
   b. .... for positive thrust.
   c. ....
   d. ....
   e. ....

3. **MY PLAN OF ACTION**
   a. .... Identify plan of action.
   b. .... Be flexible but firm.
   c. ....
   d. ....
   e. ....

4. **TIME SCHEDULE**
   a. .... Jot down your target dates.
   b. .... Achieve them one by one
   c. .... to develop confidence and
   d. .... willpower.
   e. ....

Through the foregoing idea and picture induction programme, you can make use of the energy released by your belief and faith towards achieving success.

This conscious programme turns you into the "self-making" man visualised by Dr. Sondel. He says, "To be a self-made man is commendable, but to be a self-making man is glorious".

HOW TO OVERCOME FAILURE

There are no mistakes, no coincidences,
All events are blessings given to us to learn from.

...ELIZABETH KUBER-ROSS

The word failure generally generates negative feelings. It is a hated word which conjures up negative mental images of poverty, squalor, loneliness and unhappiness.

But 90 per cent of those who fail are not actually defeated unless they quit. They see in the setback the seeds of an opportunity and evolve strategies to overcome failure and to keep going forward.

They use failure as a stepping stone to success and try to learn and reassess their approach or strategy. It is this attitude to try harder with courage and determination that makes them bounce back from failure with greater energy and ambition.

Top Achieving People (TAP) believe there is no such thing as bad luck. There is only good luck and better luck. This attitude differentiates them from quitters.

WHAT LEADS TO FAILURE

Our awareness of what holds us back enables us to take complete charge of all our faculties.

We should attempt to recognise in the following discussion the patterns of behaviour that enslave us or hold us back, and by critical evaluation and self analysis convert these into positive energies that can be harmonised for greater effectiveness towards realisation of our final goal in life.

Let us first identify the reasons for failure before we discuss the strategy to overcome it.

FEAR OF TAKING RISK

Are you afraid of doing something ? Go ahead and do it - and fear will disappear. Achievers know they have to make choices to achieve their desired goal. And a choice invariably involves risk.

Every pioneer has been a calculated risk taker. Nothing at all can be achieved by people who want to play safe. Such an attitude may at the most help a person to survive. He/she cannot make a mark in any sphere of activity.

It is said that the person who risks nothing, does nothing, has nothing and is nothing. Charles Kettering once said, "You never stub your toe standing still. The faster you go the more chance there is of stubbing your toe, but more chance you have of getting somewhere".

An Urdu poet has aptly said :

> *"Girte hain shaiswar he maidane jung mein,*
> *Woh tefil kya giray jo ghutno ke bal chale".*
>
> ...AZIM

The couplet means it is none but the brave (warriors) who fall off their horses in the battlefield. How can a child fall down that crawls on the knees.

Success involves judicious and calculated risk-taking after careful study of pros and cons. It is the outcome of one's competence, capacity for decision making and courage. It is not gambling or shooting in the dark.

> *In every work of genius, we recognise our own rejected thoughts; they come back to us with a certain alienated majesty.*
>
> **...Ralph Waldo Emerson**

You would have noticed in life that many a great idea or innovation comes about from people with courage. The meek-hearted say this idea did occur to them or they also thought likewise. But they lacked the initiative and courage to act on the idea. The truth is that people miss out on opportunities by sheer laziness and fear of taking risk.

The story goes that a farmer did not cultivate his fields one season fearing drought conditions and lack of rains. He even did not plant drought resistant corn fearing insects would eat the crop. With the result his fields remained uncultivated. This illustrates how fear of risk taking kills one's will and initiative.

The biggest steps one has to take to open up new possibilities is to risk going into the unknown.

We should not be bound by our limited past. It means we should undertake periodic sorting, and retaining from the past only that which is useful, whilst adding on that which is more effective.

Lack Of Persistence

Most people fail simply because they quit. They do not

lack knowledge or skill but they back out the moment they face a setback. Faced with the mildest of opposition, they take the easiest way out and quit.

Persistent people know they can succeed where clever and more talented people fail. They may lose their jobs, get rejected, watch their companies fail or see their ideas founder, but they take advantage of adversity, carving opportunities from it.

You have to develop a staying power in adverse circumstances to convert failure into success. Persistence enables you to work hard and prepare thoroughly towards excellence. A persistent person is a doer.

Fear Of Losing Self-Confidence

Some people accept mediocrity in life out of fear to face failure. They are scared of losing their self-confidence. They fear either being unprepared or rejection and loss of face. These persons do not try anything new. They keep to the beaten track. They remain satisfied on their home ground and do not try to venture out on unfamiliar turf. Such people lead an incomplete and unfulfilled life. It has been aptly said, "It is better to have loved and lost than not to have loved at all".

Achievers make a positive use of their fears. Fear provokes them to act positively. "Throw a man into swirling waters, his first reaction would be fear and also he would try to come out of it. To be able to face your doubts, your cowardice, it is bravery," says Shekhar Kapur, the celebrity film director.

Short-cuts To Failure

Taking short-cuts create long-term problems. It is a bad workman or a lazy, unthinking person who resorts to short-cuts which invariably lead to sorrow or loss of prestige. The straight path may be longer, the process may be time consuming but it will lead to the desired destination or goal. Short-cuts lead to production of shoddy work and loss of business.

We do come across unscrupulous persons in every organisation. These people are shirkers. They do not want to work but take full benefit of the labour of others. Such people get exposed sooner or later. They suffer loss of prestige and do not make much progress in life.

SELFISHNESS

Selfishness and greed destroy human relationships and lead to failure. Individuals and organisations that concentrate on their own benefit and have no concern for providing service or being helpful stop growing.

A selfish and self-centred person is not welcome anywhere and has no real friend.

The Bible says –

> What does a man gaineth
> if he conquereth the whole world
> But loseth his own soul.

LACK OF CONVICTION

A person lacking in conviction may go on throughout life without achieving anything. Such a person becomes a proverbial rolling stone that gathers no moss. One has to develop the courage of one's conviction to be an achiever. Our success or social contribution does not depend upon what happens to us but how we react or respond to what happens to us or around us. If our response is a positive one and we have the courage to overcome low moments in life, nothing that happens outside of us can lead to a feeling of failure or sorrow. One should not act as a mere "spectator" in life but try to be among those people "who make things happen". Persons who just stand and watch do not achieve anything.

NEGLECTING LAWS OF NATURE

Change is the law of nature. Nothing stands still. Time and tide wait for none. Everything around us is in a state of flux and change. But one must not accept change for the sake of change only. One should accept it after evaluating it. If the change is for the human good or makes for progress, it should be accepted straightway.

Again a seed has to be sown before we can reap fruit, and we reap what we sow. If we do not sow anything, we reap only weeds. This is nature's law. Similarly, our thoughts are like seeds to our mind. If we plant positive thoughts, we will develop a successful and dynamic personality of an achiever. Negative thoughts will induce negative and destructive behaviour. No man is good or bad by nature, only thinking makes it so. Thinking good and positive thoughts help in achieving our goal in life and make this world a better place to live in. But we have to continuously watch out for weeds even after planting positive thoughts. The process of weeding is a continuing one.

We must never forget that every thought we think, every word we utter, every action we perform, every feeling, every emotion

> *that wake up within us, is recorded in the memory of nature.*
> *We may be able to deceive those around us. We may even succeed in deceiving ourselves. But we cannot deceive Nature.*
>
> ....**J.P. Vaswani**

Lack Of Planning And Preparation

Lack of planning and preparation results in failure. The difference between a battle lost and a battle won is only that of preparation and planning. We all want to achieve success and be winners but very few have the will to prepare to win.

There is no substitute for preparation and planning to achieve success in any sphere of activity. Planning gives us the necessary confidence to tackle the situation head-on and achieve success.

Success has been described as 25 per cent inspiration and 75 per cent perspiration. Preparation is thus "sum total of purpose, planning, perseverance and patience", says Shiv Khera. Preparation provides us a comparatively smooth ride to success in any sphere of activity.

Lack Of Discipline

Discipline has been defined as the training of a person for proper conduct and action in all circumstances.

A disciplined person follows the positive rules in personal life and social behaviour. It is only the disciplined persons who have made accomplishments that have contributed to excellence in every sphere of human activity from science, medicine, literature and arts to sports and athletics.

A disciplined way of life generates focus and admirable self control. Arjuna, depicted as the confused person in Mahabharta, was the most focused archer of his time. His arrows always hit the bull's eye because he was not distracted like others by branches of the tree, leaves or even the body of sparrow. He saw only the eye of the bird.

Achievers learn early in their life how to harness their total energies through discipline and use these to attain their goal in life.

Making Excuses

The test of a successful man is how much he can learn and how much he can share, and how soon he confesses a mistake and makes amends for it. Achievers do analyse the reason for any failure. They do not try to find excuses; whereas losers try to rationalise and therefore do not learn from their failure. They try to blame others or the circumstances but do not look within and try to review the failure for making a renewed effort.

Thinking That Success Is An Instant Affair

Success is a constant road,
So move to new horizons.

...**Proverb**

There is no instant gratification for an achiever. Success is not an instant affair like gambling or lottery. Every achievement has a background of continuous and steady work. Once we understand that slow and steady wins the race, we do not get discouraged and are prepared to work continuously and make thorough preparation.

The story of every achievement is also a story of courage, persistence and perseverance. Abraham Lincoln faced eleven failures at different stages in life but used each failure to bounce back. He ultimately became the President of United States of America.

FATALISM

Fatalists believe that in life everything is pre-ordained and human beings are not in the driving seat. They have no control over whatever is happening to them or around them. Like Thomas Hardy's protagonists, they believe, "Life is an occasional episode of happiness in the general drama of pain".

Success for them is only a matter of luck. Such people have all the negative emotions and are weak minded. They fall easy prey to the so-called godmen and conmen.

Fatalists take up an assignment or project half-heartedly. They lack confidence and have no commitment. They are not prepared to give it their best shot.

God helps those who help themselves.

...PROVERB

One should learn early in life to accept responsibility, be a man of action and not fritter away one's energy by indulging in the negative emotion of fatalism.

TIMIDITY

> *Don't start the day with*
> *doubts and fears, for where*
> *they live, faith disappears*
>
> ...CLAY HARRISON

None but the brave deserve the fair, they say. Top Achieving People (TAP) do not look for quick-fix or easy solutions. They have the courage of their conviction to tackle the bull by the horns to achieve their goal in life. Courageous people are not cowed down by fear. They are seldom disheartened by obstacles in life and harness their positive energies to overcome the most difficult situation to make a mark in life.

> *One crowded hour of glorious life*
> *is worth an Age without a name*
>
> ...THOMAS MORDAUNT

STRATEGY TO OVERCOME FAILURE

In her book, Your Many Faces - the First Step to Being Loved, Virginia Satir says, "We all build new maps or new roadways for ourselves in our life. The inner road maps have to be resurfaced, reshaped, reconstructed and built anew. Some people make up a detailed map early and spend their lives fitting into it. Others, whom we should rather imitate, start with a large space and proceed to follow a continual process of discovery which shifts and changes the points on our map and the lines between them as we move, look, listen, speak, sort, challenge, take in and let go".

We should with patience and perseverance build up and nurture a whole network of positive attitudes which open up a whole new world of possibilities and opportunities.

Identifying our strengths and weaknesses, and dealing creatively with our fears, weaknesses, pressures and inadequacies makes available an abundant positive energy to realise our final goal in life.

We are actually defeated only if we quit. How we see a failure is entirely a function of our attitude. We have to learn from our mistakes and re-build with renewed effort.

REVIEW THE STRATEGY

If at first you do not succeed go over your planning to find out any gaps or loose ends. The strategy is not to give up but see failure as a lifeline and not a dead-end. Your perseverance and renewed preparation and planning will see you through the next time.

KNOW YOUR WEAKNESSES

We have to learn to analyse our personal weaknesses which cause failure and overcome these by self-discipline. This no doubt requires a strong willpower and self-control.

REVIEW YOUR PREPARATION AND PLANNING

An important factor in overcoming failure is to go over your preparation and plan of action once again and to make adjustments. We cannot get better result by repeating the same flawed plan.

Planning has to be reviewed with the purpose to find weaknesses and the loose ends. According to Thomas A. Edison, the inventor, our approach to planning should include – (1) ability to define what is to be achieved, (2) to concentrate our mind on the purpose, (3) to see whether all available resources have been used, (4) to take advantage of all available knowledge and to build-up on other's failures, (5) to firmly believe that there is a solution and you will find it.

GET BACK INTO ACTION

You can use failure to achieve success only if you can start all over again with renewed effort. There is much to learn from the lives of great achievers. The fear of failure did not deter them from their goal. They did not avoid action for fear of making mistakes. They used their mistakes or failures "to stretch, grow and risk", and to prepare themselves for greater success.

> *Vitality shows not only in the ability to persist but in the ability to start over.*
>
> ...F. SCOTT FITZGERALD

RECOGNISE OPPORTUNITY IN FAILURE

It is a law of life that a person who has a certain physical disability tries harder than others and develops compensating abilities to overcome the handicap. Now, for instance, I have this tinnitus (hissing sound) in one ear. Since I am aware of this disability, I am always very alert and try to make greater use of my other ear as well as my power of concentration to catch the direction of the sound and also what is being said.

For the ignorant, old age is a winter; for the achiever it is a harvest time. One has to remain alert to recognise unexpected opportunities in any failure or physical handicap. Graham Bell spent long years in developing a hearing aid for the deaf. He did not succeed but in the process hit upon the idea to develop telephone.

Failure serves as an incentive to Top Achieving People (TAP) to work harder than others. Every time they fall, they pick up something.

Start Re-Building

An achiever is not cowed down by adversity. He does not sit down and start pondering over his feelings. He just gets back into the mainstream and starts re-building his life.

Thomas Edison lost total equipment and scientific records in the fire that burnt down his laboratories in 1914.

As he stood there watching everything being reduced to ashes, he saw his son Charles who stood panic-stricken.

"Where's your mother", he shouted. "Bring her here, she will never see anything like this again as long as she lives". The next morning, going round the ashes of his hopes and dreams, the 67 years old Edison said, "There is great value in disaster. All our mistakes are burnt up. Thank God we can start anew".

This was a typical reaction of a person with a positive attitude towards life.

POSITIVE ATTITUDES OF TOP ACHIEVERS

From the foregoing we deduce the seven good habits of effective persons as follows :

- They are proactive.
- They make all their moves with the target in mind.
- They are methodical and proceed step by step.
- They think win-win.
- They are good listeners and observers.
- They are friendly and effectively relate to people.
- They are persevering. Learning is a lifelong process for them.

BASIC GUIDELINES TO AVOID FAILURE

- The quitter never wins and the winner never quits.
- Cultivate optimism and willpower.
- Keep on sharpening your skills.
- Plan, prepare and prioritise.

MOTIVATION BEGINS WITH YOU

People have needs and wants. The desire to fulfil their needs and wants motivates them into action.

Organizations and government institutions can help provide an environment which is motivating. They can give their positive guidance which helps make people think positively and to take action to fulfil their needs and wants. Positive motivation persuades people and propels them into action.

Management gurus recommend regular orientation programmes for employees to keep them motivated. Motivation, they say, is not a one shot affair. Shiv Khera in his book, "You Can Win" identifies four steps of employee motivation. He says an employee is (1) most receptive to motivation when he joins an organisation; (2) maintains his motivation level as he learns his skills and becomes productive; (3) his motivation level goes down as "he becomes an old hand and works just enough to avoid being fired"; (4) and if no corrective action of "remotivating" him is taken to bring him back to the mainstream and resume productivity, the employer is left with no choice but to fire him.

While the above analysis is downright true, the reasons for demotivation of employees cannot be reduced to a formula for the simple reason we are dealing with human beings. Demotivation can be caused by several factors like degeneration of work environment or the follow-up of introduction of new procedures or processes that are not properly explained and got accepted by the employees. Just as an army marches on its stomach and a car or bus runs on CNG or petrol and needs refuelling, in the same way an employee's productivity is directly linked to his/her motivation level which gets drained over a period of time irrespective of the fact of his being a new or an old hand. Of course the motivation level of an old hand just like fuel in an old car or bus gets exhausted faster than in a new motor vehicle.

This is the reason management experts suggest continuing motivation programmes for employees to maintain and strengthen their motivation level by recharging their batteries. These programmes, if designed thoughtfully, do achieve this objective. But, the motivation and enthusiasm thus generated does not last. Motivation should and must be an on-going process.

Employee motivation programmes are aimed at making the employees self-motivated. These inculcate in them a sense of greater responsibility and confidence and encourage them to build up a positive attitude towards work. In short, employees develop a sense of pride in their workmanship and start deriving fulfilment from their job.

Russy Mody, Chairman of TISCO says he has never read a management book in his life. His guru was the legendary JRD Tata. A few years after Mody joined TISCO in 1939, JRD sent him a note in which he pointed out that while companies paid great attention to the upkeep of their machines, little care was taken of the greatest machines of all – human beings! That, says Mody, was a lesson he never forgot.

SELF-MOTIVATION

Personal or self-motivation leads to action and generates a momentum which is invaluable for an achiever. The following tips will help you to get started –

- You have to keep on reminding yourself of the benefits of beginning a task at the earliest and the fact that well begun is half done. Reviewing the pros and cons of not starting will also help you to get started.

- DO IT NOW way of thinking will help. You may even tell friends and relatives about your goals to create an indirect pressure on you to get going.

- Break up the task into small steps and make out a schedule to achieve the goal.

- You don't have to wait for the mood or inspiration to get started. Your positive action will make you go ahead.

- Don't wait. Start the action and solutions will follow. You cannot afford to wait for the solution before you start.

WHAT MOTIVATES EMPLOYEES

Employee motivation enables organisations to get superior output from employees. The process of motivation includes

CLARITY OF COMMUNICATION

Employees seldom disobey an order. It is generally not communicated to them with clarity. This leads to confusion and lack of confidence. Communication should be simple, clear, direct and with a calm voice. According to Aksel Hoff, "dividing 100 per cent responsibility between two people gives each of them 10 per cent".

This reminds us about a story of four people who did not get clear-cut instructions. We will name them Everybody, Somebody, Anybody and Nobody. Now the boss wanted to get an important job to be done but failed to convey it with clarity to these people. Everybody was sure that Somebody would do it. Anybody could have done it but Nobody did it. Somebody got angry at this because it was Everybody's job. Everybody thought Anybody could do it but Nobody thought Everybody would not do it. It ended up that Everybody blamed Somebody when Nobody did what Anybody could have done.

Make Them Believe It

Be convincing. People are persuaded by your sincerity and depth of convictions than by your logic. Show them your commitment and they will follow you.

Build Their Self Respect – Give Them Recognition

An entrepreneur should ensure that each of his actions should build up self-respect (self-esteem) of employees. He must believe that employees want to increase productivity. This attitude gradually builds up employees' self-esteem. "Give them sincerity, give them education, give them training, give them money, give them challenge, give them job satisfaction and above all give them respect - like you expect from your superiors", say management experts.

Teach Them Discipline By Setting Example

Lead your employees with a flag in your hand. Set them a good example of discipline by your own actions. When you talk your employees will listen, and when you act they will watch you. Just as speed of the engine is the speed of the train, likewise the speed of the boss is the speed of the team.

You have to be patient and give them time to absorb your philosophy. Do not push. Pull like an engine up front. It is the most effective way when it comes to leading employees.

GENERATE FRIENDLY COMPETITION

Dale Carnegie tells the following story of a mill owner. Charles Schwab, a master motivator, was once told by the manager that the workers won't produce more despite coaxing and pushing. He just walked to the mill floor and asked the night shift how many "heats" the shift made that day. A worker told him six. He just wrote a big "6" on the floor and walked away. The next shift rubbed off "6" and wrote "7" in its place. This led to a friendly competition and the mill which had been lagging in production was turning out more work than any other mill in the plant.

GIVE THEM INFORMATION IN SMALL CAPSULES

A motivator with a view to whet the interest of the workers, releases information to them in small capsules and creates a desire to try it. He does not overload them. Give them what they can absorb. Too much information at one go de-motivates the employee. He is likely to forget it and get confused.

KNOW YOUR EMPLOYEES PERSONALLY

If you desire to motivate the employees, try to know them personally and strengthen your relationship with them. It will give you a very effective line of communication with them. Call them by name. Do know of any family problems a person may have.

LET THEM EXPERIENCE SUCCESS

Your employees' success is your success. Let them taste success. And you appreciate it sensibly and sincerely at the right time to create a snowball effect. This will encourage them and keep them going from success to success. A good entrepreneur shares his success with his employees. He gives them due recognition. It has been experienced beyond doubt that people will strive harder for recognition than for almost any other single thing in life. Genuine compliments are a form of recognition and it takes a big hearted and big thinking person to give another a compliment. This is a very powerful tool indeed.

NEW MOTIVATION STRATEGIES

The workers in the new millennium are not motivated only by increase in pay packet or promotion. They place more value on intrinsic reward which lead them to their personal goal.

Writing in the journal of Management Solutions, Dr. Gray Schuman suggests nine new motivational strategies –

- Assign an experienced pro to guide a less experienced person.
- Cross train people on each others' functional duties.
- Broaden their skills by rotating assignments.
- Broaden their contacts and expand their ability to work well with various teams.
- Encourage them to undertake special assignments.
- Encourage creative or innovative ways of handling assignments.
- Give assignments that give personal satisfaction or high visibility.
- Find out what new skills they would like to develop and then help to train them.
- Get feedback on their performance and what assignments interest them.

TECHNIQUES FOR MOTIVATION

In addition to the eight basic motivation ideas or skills, one has to use the following additional approaches to motivate people. No single approach can be used for motivating everyone.

LEAD THEM

The best approach recommended by management gurus is to be the flag bearer and lead them. People follow your example quicker than your advice. Example is the most important way in influencing people.

APPEAL TO BENEFITS

Money makes the mare go, they say. An appeal to the benefits can be used to motivate just about anyone. Only it has to be put across in such a way that people are made to feel that there are mutual benefits to both of you.

APPEAL TO EMOTIONS

This is the most powerful weapon in a motivator's arsenal. Appeal to emotions make people act quickly and with fervour. But this has to be used judiciously and in a positive manner. The purpose or the task to be achieved should be noble and contribute to organisational or social good. Again this emotional energy has to be sustained by repeated inputs otherwise it is as quick to disappear as it gets generated.

APPEAL TO NEEDS AND WANTS

There are basic human needs such as "roti, kapda or makaan" i.e., food, clothing and shelter. However, these also include the needs for love, creative expression, recognition and challenges.

APPEAL TO EXPERTISE

The appeal to a person's abilities enhances his self-worth. "You do it because you are the best at it", works wonders. People put in their best effort to seek approval.

APPEAL TO VALUES

The effect of appeal to a person's values or convictions is the most durable and lasting. People get motivated quickly because they believe it is the right thing to do, and remain motivated.

VISION

Vision is the ability to see significance of an event, idea or a development and recognize opportunity. It also refers to the ability to visualise the future.

Vision enables a person to develop a mental picture of what he/she wishes to achieve. Using this mental image as a guidepost, a person goes ahead confidently and with a sense of purpose to fulfil his/her mission in life. It is this belief in the vision that helps a person to make optimum use of the available materials and skills.

All great world leaders were visionaries. They used their vision to lead their countries to progress. Jawaharlal Nehru was one of them. He had a vision of technologically advanced modern India taking its rightful place in the world. It is the result of his vision and leadership that India is today keeping pace in all fields with the most advanced nations of the world.

SIGNIFICANCE OF VISION

Vision enables a person to develop and use his potential to the fullest. The three values of vision are – (1) it makes one's work enjoyable; (2) adds value to the work; (3) and predicts positive future and fulfilment of the vision.

LACK OF VISION

A man with vision is not born with this quality. Any person with a positive attitude who can recognise opportunities and has the courage of his conviction and commitment can be a man of vision. This quality can be cultivated by a man of action. But there are others who fail to develop this potential. Their vision may be limited because of the following factors :

NEGATIVE CONDITIONING LIMITS OUR VISION

Our past habits, our exposure to negative influences during our infancy or our negative conditioning have the potentials to limit our vision. Pavlovian Complex which induces a dog to start salivating as soon as it hears three rings of a bell, even if food is not kept in its front, shows how negative conditioning can limit our responses. Similarly habits limit a monkey's potential to pull out nuts from a narrow-mouth pitcher. A monkey puts its hand inside a pitcher and as per its habit closes the palm around the nuts it wants to pull out. It keeps the fist tight around nuts with the result fails to pull out its hand and gets caught.

We should think Big and put our potential to test by attempting bigger tasks. Practice and perseverance expand our potential. We should get rid of negative thoughts because these limit our vision.

MISTAKEN ACCEPTANCE OF OUTSIDE PRESSURES

Once you have clearly decided that your vision and your approach is valid, you should not accept outside pressure like what would others think. The story of a father and a son who took their donkey to the market is well known. Trivial and hollow criticism should not deter you from your vision.

You should not allow others to determine your behaviour. Pressure should come from inside and then you transform that into a feeling of excitement and exhilaration. Fears and pressures that most people experience are usually external. They worry about how they are going to be perceived or what people will think of them if they lose, or if they fail. When you can shed these apprehensions, you will find that competition is something to embrace and look forward to.

HANDICAPS AND PROBLEMS

Helen Keller was deaf and blind. Everyone knows how she overcame her worst handicaps to become one of the leading scholars and social workers. She could not see but she had a great vision.

The eminent physicist, and Nobel laureate, Prof. Stephen W. Hawking, suffers from a wasting disease which has caused degeneration of his nerves. His brain is functioning normally though physically he is inactive. He is the author of the best-selling book, A Brief History of Time, which has been translated in 50 languages. He has inspired people across the globe with his indomitable will in the face of acute disabilities.

History is full of great men and women who rose above their handicaps and achieved success. We should not allow our progress to be held back because of problems. We have to find a way around them to fulfil our vision. Problems are there to be overcome and vision is there to be fulfilled.

LACK OF PERSPECTIVE

To develop perspective one should change one's approach

and try to see things from a different point of view. Study of biographies of great achievers and history of other cultures also help develop our perspective. Lack of perspective is the worst enemy of one's potential.

TIMIDITY AND FATALISM

The negative belief that destiny limits our potential to achieve our vision is untrue and should be discarded. An individual can always take charge of the most frustrating situation and by sheer courage outgrow it to achieve the vision. We should not allow our current situation to rob us of our vision. Timidity and fatalism are destructive. We should turn our face towards the sun if we want to see light.

HOW TO REALISE YOUR VISION

Your positive belief that you can realise "your vision" is the most important step towards its realisation. All you have to do is to work out a strategy as follows :

DEFINE YOUR VISION

In case your vision is not crystal clear, you need to take time to meditate upon it to define and imprint it on your conscious mind. Once this is done, your determination and courage will enable you to realise it.

EXAMINE YOUR CURRENT SITUATION

You have to develop patience to work for your vision and make the necessary preparations in the light of your current situation. You will have to identify the starting point as well as the destination and decide the best way to achieve it.

BE PREPARED TO SACRIFICE OPTIONS

You will have to be prepared for sacrificing your options for the sake of achieving your vision. You have to proceed single mindedly towards your aim.

LIVE YOUR VISION - TAILOR YOUR PERSONAL GROWTH

(a) You should be prepared to make positive changes in your life to be able to fulfil your vision. This will help you in your personal growth and lead you to your vision.

(b) The pace of your personal growth will be quickened by your keeping the company of successful people. Observe them and learn from them.

YOUR BELIEF IN YOUR VISION

Build up momentum towards the achievement of your vision and develop perseverance. This will see you through to success. Continuous focus on your vision generates confidence and leads to success. People who perform the impossible believe in their own ability to do so. To perform the so called impossible requires that you have the positive conviction that it can be done fixed concretely in your mind. This belief will make everything possible. The key to success lies in the vision you hold and the strength of your conviction.

EXPECT OPPOSITION AND CRITICISM

- Be prepared for opposition. Negative thinking people who lack the motivation to have a grand dream will discourage you. Remain confident.

- Avoid the company of negative thinkers who will criticise

and discourage you. You have to maintain your commitment to your vision at all cost to realise it.

BE FLEXIBLE

Evaluate and try all new ideas while keeping your vision in focus. You may try different approaches and innovations with perseverance and persistence. You are bound to succeed.

BOOST YOUR WILLPOWER

As a preliminary step towards setting your goal and to prepare yourself thoroughly for the tasks ahead, you have to consciously develop your willpower. Top Achieving People (TAP) are men and women with tremendous willpower which they develop consciously and with effort.

We need willpower to overcome any hurdle. We need willpower to make a difficult decision and to carry it out to its logical conclusion.

We need an inner strength, a sort of attitude that makes us believe in our potential and builds up confidence to confront any challenge and to keep going.

Quite often you hear people mutter, "Oh, I just did not muster enough willpower". Well willpower is not a quality or a trait of character we are born with. It is a skill that can be developed, strengthened and directed to help you towards your objective or goal. We come across several people manifesting extraordinary strength in an emergency – a mother taking the brunt of a collapsed house on herself in the recent earthquake in Gujarat to save her child, for instance. Nothing is a barrier to us if we set our mind to it.

Italian psychologist Roberto Assagioli very aptly said long ago "Fundamental among man's inner powers is the tremendous unrealised potency of man's own will". The trained will is a masterful weapon.

According to psychologists, willpower helps people to break habits and alter their negative attitudes. People can change their lives by controlling their impulses and actions. According to Chambers Dictionary, power and control are the key words that describe willpower. The power is already there, we have only to control it. A few tips on building up willpower are as follows :

POSITIVE PURPOSE

Willpower is most effective and dynamic when applied to a worthy and extraordinary accomplishment. This enables us to break inertia and focus on the future.

HELP MAKE YOUR DECISION

Psychologists have identified four steps in making a change. These are :

(1)   Pre-contemplation (i.e. resistance to change)

(2)   Contemplation (Evaluation of pros and cons of the change)

(3)   Action (exercising willpower to make the change)

(4)   Maintenance (sustaining the change)

It has been further suggested that with a view to boost your effort you should set a deadline to serve as an additional motivating factor and be very specific and precise on the objective of your willpower. Vagueness will lead nowhere.

SEE IT AS IMAGE-BUILDING EXERCISE

Once you develop an awareness of the benefits of willpower and how these are going to improve your self image, you are motivated to go ahead and put in your best effort. Everyone wants to have control over one's life and this factor is a major will booster.

ACTING BRAVE

A positive attitude may be put up as a facade to begin with but through gradual self-motivation it can be converted into strengthening of one's willpower. This involves putting up an act as if you are strong willed and brave even if internally you feel nervous in facing a particular situation.

KEEP IT UP

A strong will becomes stronger each time it tastes success. If you successfully develop the willpower to get rid of a negative attitude or a bad habit, you gain confidence to face other challenges.

Where there is a will there is a way.

...**PROVERB**

Acting Brave builds up willpower to tackle any task

GOALS

> *The heights by great men reached and kept*
> *Were not attained by a sudden flight*
> *But they, while their companions slept*
> *Were toiling upward in the night*
>
> ...W.H. LONGFELLOW

You have by now realised the importance of right attitude blended with perfect aptitude for becoming an achiever as outlined in the foregoing discussion. This step by step process builds up your determination, courage and potential and crystalises your purpose in life.

You are fully prepared to work towards the goal or goals set for yourself. By working towards a predetermined goal, you transform yourself from one of life's spectators into a real participant.

GOALS - THE HIGHWAY TO TOP ACHIEVEMENT

Change and growth is the law of life. We all change. The people and circumstances change. So naturally the goals we set for ourselves 10 or 20 years ago need to be reviewed and changed from time to time as we go from success to success.

The process of pruning and changing continues because some goals have already been achieved and others become unrealistic because of change in circumstances and environment. These lose their relevance.

Success has been defined as the step by step realisation of a chosen goal. The significance of goals for achieving success is most invaluable. As a matter of fact, we cannot think of an achievement without a well defined goal.

More than identifying the desired end result, goals are the road map that facilitate the journey to our destination. They keep us focused and aware of where we are going, how far we have come, and how much time we have to accomplish these.

The goals we set for ourselves should be realistic and realisable. We should set goals that make us stretch ourselves to our optimum and grandest level. But don't set impossible and unrealistic goals that make the entire effort futile.

STEPS FOR SETTING YOUR GOALS

Goals are specific objectives, attained only through concrete action. "If you cannot measure it, rate it or describe it, it is probably not a goal" says Michael Leboeuf, a business consultant. High achievers know exactly where they want to go. Here are the steps to turn your goals into reality.

DEFINE YOUR OBJECTIVE

Identify and determine what you want to achieve. The goal should be measurable so that you are able to assess your progress as you go along.

WHY THE GOAL IS IMPORTANT

Defining to yourself the significance of the achievement of the goal would act as a motivator. This process will increase your chances of success.

PUT IT ON PAPER

Write down your goal on paper. This not only crystalises it in your mind but also enables you to evaluate whether your planned actions will take you towards the objective.

MAKE A LIST OF OBSTACLES AND PROBLEMS

- At this stage, against each obstacle and problem, write down your plan to solve these.
- Note down names of people and organisations who could be of help.
- Find out what further information you need.

MAP YOUR STRATEGY

When you aim for perfection in your planning, you are moving towards goal realisation. You may be miles away but moving in the right direction.

One approach could be breaking down a goal into manageable steps and attempting the first step to build-up your our confidence.

SET A DEADLINE

"A goal is nothing but a dream with a deadline," says motivational expert – Zig Ziglar. You have to identify the priorities and lay down the time schedule for different actions.

COMMIT YOURSELF

You could create an indirect pressure on yourself to carry out your deadlines by making your intention public. Now you could do that differently for varying goals. For instance, by declaring an ambitious target and making a commitment to your co-workers or boss could make you rally responses that you never thought possible.

DON'T FEAR FAILURE

Failures act as spurs for top achievers. These make them plan more meticulously and attempt courageously to attain the goal. Others might try listening to motivational audio tapes to boost their willpower.

PERSISTENCE PAYS

Persistent people know they can succeed where more clever and highly talented people fail. You may be confronted with problems on the way to a goal. Your belief in yourself and your commitment will see you through all obstacles.

IT'S NEVER TOO LATE

Age is not a barrier to achievement. As we grow older and learn more, we gain the confidence to take on new challenges. Old age is the time to harvest.

THE PURPOSE GOAL

The purpose goal is much more than a short-term or long-term goal. It is Top Achieving People's (TAPs) mission of life or a lifetime commitment.

Top achievers have the "intention and awareness" of the direction in which they are headed early in their life. They have a passion and vision that they are meant to achieve a particular goal. They are men and women with great determination and belief in themselves.

They go through the process of preliminary stage of setting short-term and long-term goals. However, in the process of putting down on paper their preliminary goals and planning and preparation for these, their main goal in life crystalises in their mind.

From this point onward they are men and women with a mission and commitment in life. They get focused on the 'purpose goal' and set their short or long term goals very carefully, always keeping in view whether these are compatible with each other and also with the main goal. They also plan in such a way that each preliminary goal serves as a step towards the achievement of the purpose goal.

ANOTHER APPROACH TO GOAL SETTING

A common sense approach to goal setting is to take three cards and write down the important areas of life - (1) Work/Studies, (2) Home/Family, (3) Personal Development - that need to be developed and cultivated in graduated steps over pre-determined periods of time with a view to achieve your main goal or Purpose Goal in life. This can be done as shown in the following flow chart :

AREAS OF LIFE

(A)　　　　　　WORK/STUDIES/TRAINING

    (a) Immediate changes/Action　...........................
    (b) Action in 4 weeks　...........................
    (c) Action for Preliminary Goal　...........................
    (d) Action for Purpose Goal

(B)   HOME/FAMILY

    (a) Immediate changes/Action   ....
    (b) Action in 4 weeks   ....
    (c) Action for Preliminary Goal   ....
    (d) Action for Purpose Goal   ....

(C)   PERSONAL DEVELOPMENT

    (a) Immediate changes/Action   ....
    (b) Action in 4 weeks   ....
    (c) Action for Preliminary Goal   ....
    (d) Action for Purpose Goal   ....

The above process will help you to develop a focus to go ahead one step at a time, thus making sure and steady progress. These activities become your strategies for success by making you always focused on your Purpose Goal.

We build our lives, a day at a time, often putting less than our best into a building and in utter disregard of the final shape of the home we are going to live in. We must have a complete mental picture of the house (i.e. our goal), if we want to live a happy and contented life. Once the house is built it is not possible to do it over. We cannot go back.

Life is a do-it-yourself project. Our attitude and the enlightened choices we make today, build the 'house' we live in tomorrow.

VALUE OF GOALS

GOALS MOTIVATE US

Your very effort to work towards your goal is the outcome of self-motivation. This drives you on to make well directed effort to achieve it. This effort, determination and will to act boosts your potential and builds up positive tension or stress to seek fulfilment in the realisation of the goal.

> *Obstacles are those frightful things*
> *You see when you take your eyes off your goal*
>
> ...**HENRY FORD**

Goals, as we have noted earlier, should be specific, realisable and measurable. Unrealistic goals reduce our motivation and lead to discouragement.

GOALS GIVE US PURPOSE

> *If you can dream it, you can do it.*
>
> ...**WALT DISNEY**

"Goals are dreams with a timetable and implementation plan", says Shiv Khera. Goals lend purpose and meaning to human life and save us from frustration. Imagine the game of hockey or football if there were no goals and no time limit. The game would be meaningless and without any purpose. Working without goals and without time limit would be meaningless. All of us are aware how while travelling by bus we keenly watch the various milestones as we pass by to keep track of our progress towards our destination.

GOALS MAKE WORK WORTHWHILE

It is human nature to value effort directed towards the achievement of a worthy goal – a goal that gives you satisfaction and an inner glow. The goal should be one which pleases others and doesn't make you end up with guilt feelings. The Bible says : What do you gain by conquering the whole world if in the process you lose your own soul.

We are often told of a person who set his heart to become president of the company he worked for. What was the use as in the process he got a divorce and his kids became drug addicts.

PRIORITISING HELPS

Very often, by prioritising, you are able to fix and refix your goals. Management people are fond of relating the following story :

The first ever employees to make a million dollar a year were Walter Chrysler and Charles Schwab in the USA. Schwab once asked a consultant to suggest how he could get more done in a day. The consultant, after spending a week with him, suggested the following :

"Every morning, write down what are the six most important things you want to do on that day. And start doing the first one first. And then the second and third. And if by then the day is gone, next day add three more. Do it for one month and if it works, send me your payment."

Schwab sent him $ 25,000.

Most of us think we are smart and start doing several things at the same time. This leads to waste of energy. "We forget that 20% of what we do will yield 80 per cent of the results and vice versa". Prioritising helps us to keep our focus right at all times.

Lack of prioritising leads to stressful thoughts. This makes us all mixed up and confused because we have not given a thought to what our goals are in our current situation or environment and how we are going to achieve these. We have not decided about our exact destination and therefore lack confidence and purpose.

GOALS HELP PERSONAL GROWTH

Goals help you to maximize potential by making you concentrate on the areas of strength and high return. You do not fritter away energy chasing meaningless or low priority goals. This helps your personal development. As a matter of fact, what you gain in terms of personal growth in the process of reaching your goal is more significant and valuable than your reaching the goal. It is this personal growth and maturity which gives you a good feeling – a feeling of self-esteem.

GOALS MAKE US "ACT IN THE LIVING PRESENT"

While you have to focus on the future to achieve your goal, yet you live, work and act in the present. You make the best possible use of the present to realise your goal. Your action in the present enables you to focus on one thing at a time, break it into small steps and accomplish the goal in fulfilment of your vision.

GOALS HELP ORGANISE IDEAS

The concentration and focus generated by goals helps us to organise our ideas and communicate these with clarity. We develop the capacity to convey complex ideas in simple terms very easily. This makes for better understanding and communication and leads to success.

GOALS PROMOTE ENTHUSIASM

Goals lift the morale of employees and give them the purpose for greater effort to achieve them. The sagging morale of employees picks up. They develop enthusiasm for working towards something tangible rather than carrying on with their daily routine and mundane tasks.

Goals Make Progress Measurable

In the process of setting our goals we break these tangible goals into small steps. This makes it very simple to keep a tab on our progress as we go ahead. This input also enables us to know that we are proceeding on the right track. This keeps up our enthusiasm and interest and makes the whole task enjoyable.

Goals Make Us Plan Ahead

Successful people plan ahead. They don't wait for others' guidance and control over their actions. It is said that a man of average abilities may bring about great changes and accomplish great tasks if he first formulates a good plan.

STAYING FOCUSED ON GOALS

There is every possibility of one's wandering off course by concentrating on unimportant things. You have to keep your eyes on your long-range goals to stay on target.

Four practical ideas given by Merrill Douglass in his book, Success Secrets, are :

- Make a list of your long-range goals
- Read your long-range goals everyday.
- Ask continually how my present actions are helping me reach my goals.
- Discuss priorities with all concerned.

DEVELOPING CORE COMPETENCIES

Competency means the quality of having suitable or sufficient skill, knowledge and experience for some purpose. It also means doing the right thing at the right time in the right way. Competency, however, does not mean "exceptional".

Competencies are the essential requirement and also the hallmark of all good managers and high performers. But what distinguishes Top Achieving People (TAP) from others is their acquisition of core competencies or even specialisation in critical operational areas. These people have a sense of pride in their workmanship and skill in execution or management of a project.

Lack of something to feel important about is almost the greatest tragedy, a man way have.
...Arthur Morgan

Top achievers carry out exceptional tasks, or turn out works of artistic and literary beauty or craftsmanship. They are not perfectionists. But they find satisfaction and fulfilment in trying to achieve perfection in everything they do. Their creativity comes from a driving force that separates a true professional from his peers. This driving force is part desire and part conscience.

Whatever your life's work is do it well. Martin Luthur King, Jr. says, "If it falls to your lot to be a street sweeper, sweep street like Michelangelo painted pictures, like Shakespeare wrote poetry, like Beethoven composed music; sweep streets so well that all the hosts of heaven and earth will have to pause and say, 'Here lived a great street sweeper, who swept his job well.'"

When talent combines with conscience, the result can be awesome. The gifted pianist, Ignacy Paderewski, was once asked why he practiced six hours a day when he was at the peak of his career.

"If I miss one day's practice, I notice, he replied.

"If I miss two days the critics notice. If I miss three days the audience notices."

Top Achieving people (TAP) are naturally blessed with positive attitudes or they develop these quickly by observation, inclination and self-indoctrination. They have a feeling that they are destined to make a mark in life and accomplish their grand dreams. They are men and women with 'a mission' in life. This right attitude blended with perfect aptitude enables them to develop core competencies required for the achievement of the goal.

These competencies are generally acquired and developed by them during general education or professional education of B-Schools or IITs. TAP people have an open mind. They keep on learning and are most receptive to new ideas.

' In today's competitive environment, each day young professional graduates pose a threat to the other practising and professionally successful ones. Competition is continually rising, threatening to overtake the mediocre professionals. In this scenario, it is only the fittest who will survive.

The young achievers continue to sharpen their competencies during their work experience. It is here, during practical work environment, they find out their particular strength areas. They develop these areas or core competencies by innovating new products, experimenting with new ideas or formulating new procedures or policies. They keep abreast of what's happening in their field.

They are always ready to work in new areas within an organisation or even in different locations in or outside the country to pick up and develop new competencies which provide them an over-view of the operations of the organisation.

Since their eyes are set on the top rungs of the corporate ladder they aren't satisfied with looking at the working of the organisation in parts like the five blind men who went about exploring an elephant. They are like the sixth man who flew in a helicopter to have an over-view.

They are fast learners and men and women of action. They pick up, learn and practice new and relevant ideas and technologies and analyse whether these would suit their particular requirement and the prevailing environment. They are equally willing to share their knowledge and skill with others to help them realise their chosen goals.

Top Achieving People develop practical wisdom. They do not just see the obvious ; they observe everything carefully, have a practical approach and develop trouble shooter or problem solving competency.

When all think alike, no one thinks very much

...**Walter Lippman**

Top Achieving People (TAP) are farsighted and men and women with a vision. They are able to see beyond the obvious. They have the special competency of asymmetrical thinking. They are not bound by set patterns.

> *When patterns are broken,*
> *New worlds can emerge.*
>
> ...Tuli Kupferberg

The above exceptional competencies of having an overview, farsightedness and asymmetrical thinking equip them with on the spur decision making capability which is the hallmark of Top Achieving People (TAP). In the current e-environment, when available response time is very limited, quick decision makers will always carry the day.

COMPETENCIES FOR LEADING FROM THE SIDE

Management guru Peter Duckers says "you have to learn to manage in a situation where you don't have command authority, when you are neither controlled nor controlling". This kind of situation has been defined as "leading from the side".

It has been confirmed by various management surveys that generally effective managers preferred management by persuasion rather than by issuing orders, says J.A. Cogner of Leadership Institute of the University of Southern California's business school.

You have leadership competency if others respect you, seek your advice and value your suggestions. Leadership, according to Cogner, is not a matter of having a title, it comprises a few attributes and attitudes that distinguish a person from others.

These attitudes and attributes according to J.A. Cogner, include : (1) your reputation for hard work and integrity; (2) your capacity to introduce new facts or insights in a meeting or a brainstorming session; (3) your way of interaction with people i.e., eliciting inputs from others by asking questions as part of a solution". This would mean synergising. Again you could lead others by setting an example by your own conduct and behaviour thus projecting yourself as a role model.

In addition to the foregoing attributes, the following competencies are recommended by Fisher and Sharp which focus on your research, analysis and application of mind to a project :

- You could establish your leadership by "suggesting the need for setting up goals and then help in drafting these."
- Go fully prepared to a meeting by collecting the necessary data; "raise relevant issues, analyse situation and propose action based on this analysis."
- You could be generally helpful to your colleagues and extend genuine appreciation of a good job done.

ROLE OF HRD PROGRAMMES

The current increasing job mobility, reducing hierarchy, ethics and interpersonal communications have focused the Human Resource Development's (HRDs') attention on employee retention. They have set up programmes for upgrading and optimising the human capital.

These orientation and HRD programmes assume all the more importance in view of the fast changes in technology environment and innovation in products affecting consumer market.

Top Achievers enthusiastically join all such in-house programmes or even avail themselves of corporate sponsored programmes of training in specialised institutions in India or abroad to update and sharpen their competencies.

Improving and building up competencies is a continuing effort of Top Achieving People. They do not slacken their effort on accomplishing their goal. They continue to work towards new horizons. And this is what distinguishes their mental make-up from others.

From the foregoing we may sum up that competencies include things like – (1) leadership (2) team work (3) conscience, (4) pride in one's management capability, or workmanship, (5) practical wisdom, (6) far-sightedness, and (7) the ability to stand up for your beliefs. According to Prem Kamath of Hindustan Lever Limited (HLL), each competency is defined over work levels and gets consistently more strategic in nature as managers rise through work levels.

There is no fixed formula or requirement of particular competencies for various tasks, jobs and professions. The gurumantra is doing the right thing at the right time in the right way or right direction. The requirement of core competencies differs from job to job, level to level (i.e., manager, product manager, CEO), and profession to profession. Top Achieving People (TAP) are able to rise to the occasion in any situation. They are totally organised from within. They have right attitudes and perfect aptitude blended with a driving force that is part passion and part compulsion to excel.

TIME MANAGEMENT

Time is money. Every minute costs. Once you become habitually conscious of this, you learn to manage your time better. You also start realising how much more work or how many more tasks you are able to attend to by managing your time. Achievers distribute their time judiciously to different tasks in life.

Time management also enables you to concentrate on productive tasks or things which have to be done. I call this TTM i.e. Total Time Management.

WHERE TIME GOES

In order to learn time management, you have first to find out where time goes and drastically reduce wasteful activities.

What Wastes Time
- Frequent meetings without any agenda.
- Unprofessional conducting of proceedings of meeting
- Lack of organisation or over organisation in office work leads to misplacing of things or render these inaccessible. Albert R. Karr's survey of 200 companies reveals that executives waste nearly one-tenth of their time looking for misplaced items.

FREQUENT INTERRUPTIONS

Dr. Larry Baker of Time Management Centre Inc. opines that interruptions during work are "twice damaging". Besides the time taken by the actual interruption, it also takes additional time of the person interrupted to refocus on his/her work. Frequent interruptions are the result of following factors :

- Lack of Total Time Management (TTM).
- Lack of clear instructions to others.
- Procrastination - Postponing timely decisions. "Nothing is so exhausting as indecision, and nothing so futile", says, Bertrand Russel.
- Sheer Laziness - One should overcome laziness and become organised by

   (a) using a planner (b) changing work setting to develop a focus (c) punctually starting the day early.
- Plan ahead to take care of unexpected delays.
- Failing to solve a problem : Instead of wasting your time on a problem that defies solution at the moment, you wait for the right time when you can solve it by collecting the requisite information. In this way you prevent yourself from acting before appropriate time.
- Personal negative attitudes : Emotional disturbance can cause loss of productive energy. Develop positive attitude and avoid defensiveness and jealousy.
- Lack of Priorities : Listing one's priorities is the most important time management skill that deserves keen attention.

3Rs OF DETERMINING PRIORITIES

Start the day with a clear picture of how you should be spending your time. Do that by asking questions on 3 Rs.

1). What is Required of you ?
2). What gives highest Return?
3). What gives greatest Reward?

3Es OF FOCUSING ON PRIORITIES

1) Evaluate - (what is to be done)
2) Eliminate - (superfluous tasks)
3) Estimate - (time frame for accomplishment of goal)

Concentration and Visualisation of success makes you a winner.

MANAGING STRESS

Stress is a dominant factor of modern living with its fast pace and high pressure. There is a ceaseless pursuit of amassing wealth and creature comforts of life. We do not spare a thought whether or not these are contributing to our happiness, good health or peace of mind.

The fast pace of change keeps people high strung and leaves them with little time for themselves or their families. This disruption in family life today is a major source of stress.

Again there is little peace for people at work place. Competitive environment, demanding schedules, and the ceaseless hum and vibrations caused by interactive electronic tools, that keep people on call every moment of their life, make them edgy and stressful.

We are being driven into a rat race for success without learning to master and channelise our positive energies to build healthy relationships at work place. This leads to adverse effect on our mental and physical health and builds up stress. Besides ill health, stress also takes the joy out of life that we seek so eagerly.

Stressful situations can come from many factors that result in negative emotions of anxiety, anger, greed, insecurity, lust or jealousy.

Psychologists warn people against activities that go to build stress. Stress has emotional, behavioural and psychological as well as cognitive repercussions, often affecting adversely our qualities of empathy and compassion for others.

CREATIVE STRESS IS INSPIRING

Stress is a powerful force which can either be creative or harmful. A certain kind of positive stress is equated with creative tension. This may be called mother of achievement. This inspires human beings to fulfil their grandest dreams. Positive stress can actually be enriching and performance boosting. All great achievers experience their quota of such creative stress or tension which goes into turning them into TAP.

It is creative stress that generates great perseverance, persistence and determination in great achievers to continue with their efforts despite repeated setbacks. Thomas Edison failed 10,000 times before he succeeded in inventing an electric bulb.

It is this stress that has been at the back of all great works of art, literature and science. It was William Wordworth who acknowledged that his poetry was the result of "a spontaneous outburst of powerful feelings".

Again it is this kind of stress that makes men and women do great acts of bravery and even lay down their lives in the service of humanity or their country.

But generally too much stress or continuous tension that one cannot control is harmful and destructive.

HOW TO DEAL WITH STRESS

EFFECT OF STRESS ON ATTITUDES

The adverse effects of stress are reflected in following behavioural changes :

- Overreaction to events, circumstances and in interaction with others makes one unsure of one's judgement and liable to make mistakes or prone to accidents.

- Overdependence on tranquillisers which leads to loss of zest for living.

- Overindulgence in alcohol, smoking or overeating. This creates loss of self-image and leads to a feeling of inferiority complex and lack of confidence.

The overall effect of the above attitudinal changes is very damaging to one's personality.

KINDS OF STRESS

Dr. H. Selye has identified four kinds of stress :

These are - (1) Understress - which leads to boredom and a feeling of listlessness and hopelessness ; (2) Over stress- which makes one think one has to (or needs to) push beyond one's limit; (3) Eustress - which is associated with creative and positive things and (4) Distress - which is the result of pent up and unresolved anger, fear or frustration.

Stress is thus caused by how we interpret and react to events. We have to plan our life and work in such a way as to avoid stress.

Worrying about too many things causes stress. Different corporate and general public surveys conducted in USA reveal a general trend showing that almost 92 per cent of the people worry unnecessarily about hypothetical events and situations. Also people do not prioritise their daily activities and try to take on a cocktail of activities which cause stress. The surveys also reveal that less than one-tenth of the people's worries are "legitimate".

Continuous stress is harmful. You have to try to relieve it by training your mind to overcome stress and lead a style of life that does not create it. Top Achieving People are always in full control of themselves by training and inclination. They develop a totally self-integrated personality which makes them stress resistant.

ATTITUDINAL SELF ANALYSIS

We learn from the foregoing that training our mind to remain stress free is the critical factor in leading a stress free life. It is our own attitude which fuels stress and it is our attitude alone that can guard us against it.

The key to deal with stress lies in paying attention to it and to examine its effects. Edward M. Hallowell, psychologist and author of the book, "Worry : Hope and Help for a Common Condition", says you can develop stress resistance by analysing, "Is the worry leading to constructive productive action or is it paralysing you, wasting your energy".

You should find time to analyse your unconscious as well conscious mind to find out the root cause i.e., whether stress is caused by your incompetence at the conscious or unconscious level or it is caused by your competence at the conscious or unconscious level, says Dr. H. Selye.

Having analysed the root cause you should adopt strategies to deal with your stress related attitudes - (1) Find what behaviour of yours is causing it i.e., become aware of it ; (2) Now think how to overcome or change it or see how to develop a refocus on the problem; (3) Stop being tense.

STRATEGIES TO DEAL WITH STRESS

People with positive attitudes develop their own strategies to become stress resistant. We are also advised by experts of different methods to beat stress. You will however find a single thread running through various tips discussed here :

Kiran Bedi, author, sociologist and Megasaysay award winner, recommends the following five tips to beat stress :

(a) Do not scheme against others : Avoid plotting and scheming against others; it will only disturb you.

(b) Don't overwork yourself : Never overwork yourself. It saps your energy and actually can be mentally tiring as well.

(c) Count your blessings : If you are in the habit of counting your blessings and not your inadequacies, you can possess what money cannot buy. Work on your shortcomings and try to improve yourself.

(d) Be yourself : Don't compare yourself with others and don't dwell on your inadequacies. That will only make you suffer from an inferiority complex. Learn to accept yourself as you are.

(e) Be grateful : Be positive and learn to spread happiness around you. Focus on what you have, that will give you more mental peace (i.e., life without stress) :

Based on psychologists recommendations, we have compiled the following comprehensive guidelines to avoid stress :

PRIORITISE YOUR GOALS TO CONQUER STRESS

By prioritising your goals, you get a chance to review your goals and this reduces stress. The incident of Schwab and the consultant narrated earlier is the best example of prioritising of our daily activities to avoid stress.

Let me tell you of my personal experience : My stress level has decreased because I am no longer constantly trying to remember what I have to do a few days ahead. Now I just pull out my planner, see the schedule and am all set for the day. When I get stressed out, I look at my schedule and find I still have plenty of time to catch up on all tasks.

One of the few things that cannot be recycled is wasted time. So why not plan ahead. This saves you time and keeps you stress free.

BALANCE DEMANDS AND RESOURCES

Stress is also the result of mismatch between demand and available resources. You have to balance the two either by reducing your demands or increasing your resources to avoid stress.

In the course of his evolution, man's needs too have evolved into a mind boggling range of cravings. The greater the human population has grown, the greater is the magnitude of its self-centeredness and more grave the consequences of its endless pursuit for the fulfilment of these cravings. This confounded state is described by Buddhism as "tangles within and tangles without" and people are enmeshed in these tangles leading to a highly stressed life.

Do Your Best And Be Ready For The "Best"

The most damaging thing one can indulge in is worrying. And worrying about risk freezes one's initiative and leads to total ineffectiveness. We should face risks confidently, put in our wholehearted and very best effort and remain free of stress.

Have A Proper Perspective

The present circumstances or situation should be seen with reference to the larger picture to develop a proper understanding to deal with it. This will keep us stress free. Perspective has been defined by Earl Wilson as "the ability to see the present moment and immediate events against the background of a larger reference".

Work In Your Areas Of Strength

In order to avoid stress and be able to put in your very best effort, you should work in the areas of your strength. Your areas of strength are those wherein even if you make mistakes or fail, you do not feel threatened or dejected; rather these offer you a challenge to do your best to succeed. The opposite is true of weaknesses which make you feel tense and threatened.

Avoid Rat Race

The present competitive environment has been described as rat race. There is an intense and irrational competition between people in the business world. This leads to unnecessary stress. We should be competitive and work hard to achieve our goal but it should not be at the cost of our health, family life or people we work with.

CONVICTIONS KEEP STRESS AT BAY

Every success has been a story of strong convictions of truly successful persons. It is these convictions that provide them with the motivation and the willpower to succeed and also to remain stress free.

> *I do not think that winning is*
> *The most important thing. I*
> *Think winning is the only thing*
>
> ...BILL VEECK

DO NOT TAKE ON MORE THAN YOU CAN HANDLE

Prioritise your tasks and take on only what you can handle and complete. Start solving one problem at a time. Look at an hour glass in which only one particle goes through at a time and apply this idea to your problems. Again think and try a new approach or find a better way to solve these problems.

KEEP EMOTIONS UNDER CONTROL

You should monitor your thoughts and choose only the positive. In other words control your thoughts before they control you. Stay away from negative thoughts and remain stress free.

HELP OTHERS : LOOK OUTWARD

Too much and continuous self-focus often leads to restlessness and discouragement. This is so because you cut yourself off from the mainstream of life. This causes stress. Look around. Help others and be aware of the less fortunate brothers and sisters. The happiness that we give to others comes back to us. The happiness that goes out travels back as it moves in a circle.

LEARN TO RELAX

You may learn music, arts or read good inspirational books, play golf or attend the neighbourhood satsang. This will give you energy to get back to business with renewed energy.

Music therapy has been found to be particularly effective in providing relaxation. Studies have found it effective as an analgesic and anxiety reducer.

Meditation is a self-directed practice for relaxing the body and calming the mind. The primary purpose of meditation has been religious although its good effect on health has long been recognised. During the last 15 years, it has been explored as a stress reducer for both mind and body and is often recommended as a way to lower blood pressure. Studies have shown that meditation strengthens the immune functions by lowering stress hormone levels.

PHYSICAL STRATEGIES

You should seek pleasant company, good environment, fresh air; take plenty of water and practice silence; visualize yourself as a stress free person; develop hobbies and interests other than your work.

Light physical exercise, yoga and deep breathing will help relieve stress. But get your blood pressure checked before undertaking any exercise.

Unfurl your sails

Rise above the mind body complex in a quality solitude time for a few minutes to handle stress. Develop faith in yourself and a general helpful attitude towards others to achieve a richer fuller life.

PART-II

INTERACTIVE SKILLS

Synergy Action : A committed team in a synchronised action can achieve the so called impossible.

Synergy Action : A committed team in a synchronised action can achieve the so called impossible.

RELATIONSHIPS

Success is knowing how to get alongwith people
...ELEANOR ROOSEVELT

People are the most important, dominant and all pervading factor in all spheres of life. Our life on earth has meaning only in relation to others.

Top Achieving People (TAP) are keenly aware of the important role of others in their achievement. In addition to developing the right attitude., they have a special knack of getting along with other people. They are PR people par excellence. They build human relationships and consider these to be the building blocks of life.

The ability to deal with other people or to get along with them is the most important human characteristic. Whatever be one's profession or occupation, in daily life one has to deal with one's spouse, children, neighbours, co-workers, employees, superiors or the boss.

It is said good human relationship like charity begins at home. The positive quality of our relationships at home and with neighbours lays the foundation of our attitudes. The following guidelines will help in building relationships at all levels in life :

Make Caring Your Target

The following poem sums up everything that caring represents. As a matter of fact this could be considered a gurumantra of human relationships :

> *Caring is loving,*
> *listening and accepting*
> *Caring is communicating,*
> *understanding and respecting.*
> *Caring is openness,*
> *sensitivity and availability*
> *Caring is supporting,*
> *promoting and responding.*
> *Caring is cooperating,*
> *participating and sharing.*
> *.... ....*

...George Kaitholil

Caring is the foundation of good relationships. A survey of 16,000 executives published by Wall Street Journal recently shows that 13 per cent identified as Top Achieving People (TAP) cared as much about people as they did about profits.

Know Them Intimately

Remembering a person's name leaves the most positive effect on him/her and goes a long way in building relationships. This is all the more so if a person in authority remembers the name of the people working for him/her.

The quality to know and take sincere interest in your employees' and casual acquaintances' problems is the most important characteristic to be found among army generals and successful entrepreneurs all over the world. This builds up an intimate comradeship between them and the men. The men start looking upto the chief as a father figure and are prepared to put in their best effort irrespective of the fact whether it is a battlefield or a production unit. It is important for the person in authority to take interest in the people who work with him/her and spend time, emotion and money on them.

BUILD CREDIBILITY

The basic foundation of good relationship is credibility. All human relationships, families, friends and organisations need trust to function effectively. One's positive attitude and genuine interest in others earns him / her trust of others with ease. Top achievers deliver more than they promise and automatically establish credibility and trust of clients, colleagues and others. Lost credibility results in loss of friends; it also destroys business relationships.

EACH PERSON COUNTS

Each person you meet is a person of consequence. Meeting people one at a time affords a unique opportunity to make a lasting impact and build a durable relationship. This enables your goodwill to be built-up by word of mouth.

Each one of us is unique and different, yet we need each other for a full experience of life. The attention and courtesy shown to others make this world a better place and enable us to effectively synergise with others.

CONSULT THEM SEEK ADVICE

Your positive attitude to consult other people makes for building and nurturing positive relationships besides giving you an opportunity to know what they think. Asking for a favour has a similar impact. People relate it to your humility and respect you.

When we accept and welcome one another, we also grow with one another. We feel safe to open up and share our problems and failures and weaknesses. Such sharing will only enhance the bond of unity and mutual support among us.

GIVE AND TAKE ATTITUDE HELPS

The positive attitude to build-up your relationship with others through give and take is most fruitful. Their is nothing more important in life than helping the other person to achieve his / her goal. This positive attitude can help you grow more self-supportive and promote self-realisation by bringing your potentialities into bloom.

BE CONSIDERATE TO OTHERS FEELINGS

"Give me the right word and the right accent, and I will move the world", says novelist Joseph Conrad. I am reminded of the story told to me about a garment store in Moscow's Leninsky Prospect which carried the signboard "BIG SIZES" in Russian language. Obviously the store did not attract many customers. People did not even go in to have a look at the merchandise. The moment the management changed the signboard to "BIG PEOPLE", the sales picked up.

BE A GOOD LISTENER

Good listening is a part of availability. It means you give your time and attention to the other person. It shows you are interested in understanding that person as correctly and completely as possible.

The following is a summary of suggestions by PR experts :
- Stop talking

- Empathise with the speaker. Put yourself in the speaker's shoes and find out what he is trying to convey.
- Concentrate. This will focus your attention on his/her words, ideas and feelings and not on your response.
- Look at the person – his / her body language.
- Smile and nod appropriately. Don't overdo it.
- Get the main points and the thrust of what is said.
- Don't antagonise the speaker.
- Leave your emotions behind. Try to check your own worries. These are bound to distract you.
- React to ideas and not to persons.
- Avoid hasty judgments.
- Ask questions. This will help clarity in understanding.
- Evaluate facts and evidence. Try to identify not only the significance of the facts and evidence, but how they are related to arguments.
- Avoid jumping to assumptions. This will interfere with your listening and the ability to understand.
- Recognise your own prejudice.
- Identify the type of reasoning. The listener should make every effort to learn to spot faulty reasoning.
- Give accurate feedback. This can be done by paraphrasing or reflecting on what you just heard. It becomes a relatively easy process with practice.

PROVIDE SERVICE

The purpose of human life is to be of service to others. This builds up positive and lasting relationships. This has a very important application in the competitive business world. Customers are attracted to a store for its credible after sales service even if the product offered is comparatively expensive.

Jim Dornan in his book, Success Strategies, analyses that two out of three customers that you lose leave because they are dissatisfied with the service.

TALK ON WHAT INTERESTS THEM

By focusing on other peoples'. interests rather than your own, you can build a positive relationship. Encourage the other person to talk about himself/herself.

MAKE THEM FEEL IMPORTANT

There is nothing more important than people. We build lasting relationship by giving them genuine praise and respect. A sales person who is able to do that makes the sale.

AVOID ARGUMENTS

Discussion is healthy and mentally enlightening and beneficial. But arguments are negative; they represent a forceful attempt to change a person's point of view. Management experts and successful entrepreneurs have developed the following guidelines to resolve a disagreement while building positive relationship :

- **Welcome disagreement** : You may benefit by considering the disagreement as an opportunity to be corrected before a serious mistake is committed.

- **Discard immediate reaction to defend yourself :** Maintain your composure and think before you give your first reaction.
- Control your temper
- **Listen first :** Do not resist or defend. It will raise barriers to communication.
- **Look for areas of agreement :** Build rapport on the basis of areas of agreement and then proceed to find a solution on this common ground.
- **Be Honest :** Admit mistakes, if any, and apologise for these. It will reduce the other person's defensiveness and provide an opportunity to find a positive solution.
- **Promise to think over and study the idea :** Don't put yourself in a position to ignore the other person's ideas and get into trouble. Tell him/her you will study the idea and sincerely do it.
- Thank sincerely for his/her interest.
- Hold action/decision to enable you both to think over the problem.

The above guidelines offer good strategy to thrash out a positive solution to any difference of opinion. These allow you to admit when you are wrong and recommend the use of great tact in your approach to change the other persons point of view. If possible you may help him believe that he first thought of the idea and repeat the remarks that are in line with your point of view. Tell how the change will evidently help in view of the changed environment or circumstances.

- **Observe and Learn :** In order to develop a better understanding of the people you meet, you should try to know their fears, hopes and dreams. This will help you build positive relationships with people. This faculty will specially be helpful to sales persons in insurance and security agencies to make use of these positive fears to sell their services.

NETWORKING AND INTERNET

Networking is nothing but group relationships aimed at pooling social, professional and business resources to achieve our goals in life. Good relationships with associates, colleagues, superiors and others are highly valuable. You cannot command good relationships; these have to be nurtured and built by taking genuine interest in people with whom we work. Positively used networking helps all the participants or the group of people to achieve their goals and in the process contribute towards total human development.

Top Achieving People (TAP) are adept at positive networking. They also make use of internet and other information technologies to advance the group's common objectives.

Networking operates at three levels :

(a) Social Networking
(b) Professional Networking
(c) Inter-Business Networking

We shall consider each briefly :

SOCIAL NETWORKING

Social Networking has been going on ever since human

life came into existence. Animals and birds of feather have been "living and flocking" together in groups. The primitive man also lived and moved around in groups for security and support.

As populations in different areas of the world grew and groups started drifting to other places for water, food and other resources, it was networking which kept these groups together and maintained their identities.

Looking nearer at today's small social and religious groups, we can safely conclude that these have come into existence to maintain and safeguard their identities and for building up support and security among the members. It becomes most convenient and viable among these social groups to find matches for their daughters and sons, share in each others happiness and sorrow, and to economically help build-up the entire group. Social networking has been going on since times immemorial and TAP people have used it with positive results.

PROFESSIONAL NETWORKING

This has got a tremendous boost through internet and use of Information Technology. Fast and tremendous progress in science, medicine, arts, literature and education has made it almost impossible for professionals to keep track of the developments in their field within the country and outside.

Man has gone global in thinking and is not content merely with updating knowledge. Everyone wants to know, understand and apply the latest and the recent development.

The use of internet has further fueled the professional's urge to be proficient. This, however, has not been a one-way affair. The achievers among the professionals are equally keen to put their achievements and discoveries on the internet to claim instant credit for their work as well as share it globally.

We learn of a recent case of 5-year old Sonia who was suffering from a serious and rare neurological disorder. There appeared to be no hope. The parents felt very frustrated and miserable. At this time a young resident doctor told them of electronic communities on the Net. This led to an immediate search for a community of neurologists.

They found the community and also got a ray of hope for Sonia's case in that group. Sonia's case became a topic of discussion of neuro-surgeons all over the world. And today, thanks to access to this facility on the Net, she is almost cured.

These communities on the internet exist in the form of clubs where people with similar interests form a group and help not only each other but also try to find a solution to any problem referred to them.

NETWORKING HELPFUL TOOL FOR ACHIEVERS

Networking Has Become A Very Helpful Tool For Top Achievers – (1) to develop contacts and maintain them; (2) to spread the good word or good deed around and build PR; (3) to encourage give and take without keeping a ledger of debits and credits; (4) to learn of the latest and the best in their sphere of activity; (5) to make greater effort for achievement in their field and to put it on the internet at the earliest for fast dissemination of new ideas and procedures; (6) to share their specialisation with others and help upgrade the professionals all over the world; (7) to practically demonstrate medical and technological advances and consult others in finding solutions to health or other problems.

In short TAP individuals have been using the limitless benefits of networking for themselves and the human society as a whole. It is the most important tool for success in today's context when interdependence is of greater value than independence.

INTER-BUSINESS NETWORKING

This is used at various levels. But the two relevant levels for our discussion are : (a) Inter-Organisation Networking and (b) Global Corporate Networking.

INTER-ORGANISATION NETWORK

CEO's and efficient managers within an organisation carefully build up inter-organisation networking with their colleagues and share their experience and suggestions to increase the smooth flow of communication within the organisation and to help motivate everyone. This builds up a sense of pride in the organisation and its product and leads to overall increase in competency and productivity.

They also make positive use of networking to maintain continuing communications with the various publics like customers, clients, suppliers, distributors and others.

Networking is used by TAP people to keep themselves informed of what their competition is upto and keeping ahead of it. They would, for instance, know when a new line of garments or shoes is going to be introduced and who are the target customers.

GLOBAL CORPORATE NETWORKING

In today's fast and ever changing market trends, the role and skills associated traditionally with business leadership are not enough. Leadership paradigms are evolving with the changing dynamics of business, says Pallab Dutta, of Hindustan Lever Ltd., writing in the Economic Times. He says :

"Today's business leadership makes extensive use of networking in its effort for excellence in everything they do. The leader evaluates complex information, engages in working relationships with counterparts across space and time, keeps tab on world market and tries to be innovative or different."

Corporate leaders have taken full advantage of networking by developing bold new e-vision suited to their particular line of business. This has enabled them to excel in the faster execution of well-chalked out growth and address the needs of the global market place. They have kept hawk-like watch over developing international situation and how it would affect the supply of raw materials or the sale of their products. For instance, any major crisis among oil producing countries could have a ripple effect on the world economy.

INTERNET

INFORMATION ANY TIME ANYWHERE

The fast growth of internet has made information "any time anywhere" a reality. Added to this are the host of new appliances in the pipeline that will enable you to see the digital image of the person you are talking to and hear his/her voice. Digital content is dynamic; it allows interaction, and it is customizable. This coupled with wireless communication and broad band access will be the key technologies that bring information and content to the people.

Top Achieving People (TAP) will not have to be hardware engineers or top class computer programmers. They would learn how to use the new technologies. They would acquire the expertise to use effective conversational language and symbols that are understood globally. They would know the strengths and weaknesses of the medium and exploit it to the fullest to get the maximum benefit.

IMPACT OF INTERNET INFORMATION

The use of internet will have a far reaching effect on our total way of life as follows :

GLOBAL POWER, REACH AND INTERACTION

You will go global in your thinking, expand your horizon and develop a global perception. This will bring a positive change in your outlook and stimulate your vast potential for excellence.

Most of us go through life only "half awake" said William James. But in actual practice people use only one-third of their potential. Internet communication and its possibilities will stimulate you enough to sit-up and explore the tremendous power, reach and interactive elements of the internet.

INCLUSIVE VISION

TAP individuals will be stimulated by the power and reach of internet to make the optimum use of their inclusive vision. They would be able to exchange their thinking and ideas on a larger human canvas. Again this would enable them to get the best out of the people they work with and generate positive energy and enthusiasm to achieve their goal. Internet will thus help Top Achievers to build-up team working on a wider scale.

THINKING BEYOND THE OBVIOUS

Internet interaction will make you feel more confident and

in self-control. It will unleash your positive mental energy to think Big, think beyond the obvious and be innovative. This positive quality has contributed to all great discoveries, inventions and works of art. All great achievers were marked by immense curiosity to look beyond the obvious to achieve their grand goals. And this is exactly what distinguishes Top Achieving People (TAP).

TLDs Will Encourage Excellence

Internet top-level domains (TLDs) such as .com and .org will help users to locate websites in their chosen fields of interest and help them build up their expertise. This will encourage excellence. People will be stimulated to learn more and more as aptly put in the following lines of the poet :

To follow knowledge like a sinking star,
Beyond the utmost bounds of human thought.

...Homer

Promote Sharing And Exchange Of Information

Top Achieving People (TAP) will find fulfilment in sharing and exchange of information, ideas and expertise. These positive qualities would enable them to develop synergy for self-growth and the progress of human society as a whole.

Promote Wealth Creation Of Society

Top Achieving People will be able to make an effective use of the internet technology not only for their personal achievements but also for tapping the wealth creation capability of our society by making individuals and manufacturing processes highly productive.

APPROACH TO ANYTIME ANYWHERE INFORMATION

Achievers use positive and appropriate words in their spoken or written communication on the internet. They adapt words to time, place, occasion and even to people of different nationalities in their interactions on the internet.

They develop selling phrases, courtesy phrases, warm, friendly and enthusiastic words and phrases in their interaction on the internet to win friends and influence people.

The following tips on the approach to internet communications has been recommended by experts :

1. **Speed :** The most essential requirement in the new e-environment is speed in all spheres of activity–speed in sorting out information, speed in reaction and decision, and speed in action. MIT Media Laboratory's head, Mr. Schrage, reflects thus – "Production cycles grow shorter, consumers expect service around the clock ; companies do things in parallel that they would once have done sequentially." All this requires greater speed and efficiency.

2. **Need of Team Workers :** More than ever today the companies need fewer but better people who can work as a team. These people with new talents, skills and attitudes will comprise "celebrity teams".

3. **Openness :** There will be a greater transparency allowing your partners, suppliers or consumers total access to your database and inner workings. This will require a great deal of confidence and trust to allow everyone to know your weaknesses and mistakes.

4. **Collaboration Skills :** A whole lot of new opportunities will emerge to enable teams and companies to work together. The teams may be separated by time zones or geographic distance or they may be working for different employers.

5. **Discipline :** Internet will encourage much greater discipline than what we are used to. "The Internet is all about discipline, protocols and standard processes," says Mr. Britan of U.T.C.

6. **Primacy of Customer :** "Today product and process has taken a back seat and companies have to focus on the customer to provide him/her customized product and service. Experts insist that this shift has come about with the primacy of Internet Communications."

INTERNET WILL SHAPE OUR FUTURE INTERACTIONS

We have till this day seen only one-tenth of the impact of internet. The number of uses and services are going to grow phenomenally and achievers will take full advantage of this powerful medium.

Michael Derlouzas, Director of MIT laboratory for Computer Science says :

"....the big changes will be felt through technological capabilities, usage patterns and social consequences still to come.

"Qualitatively, we are somewhere around a tenth of the web's or internet's full potential. We can look forward to speaking to our machines and unloading our work on them. Today we do everything ourselves, taxing our eyes and brains. While content is always on the tip of our tongue, we ignore information work which is ten times bigger."

According to S. Ramachand, CEO Tata consultancy, "The internet paradigm is ...all about global collaboration in terms of communication connectivity and partnership on a scale yet unprecedented. We need to embrace this in everything we do, whether these are internal systems or our own efficiencies, knowledge-gathering, dissemination communication with each other and use this as a medium more than anything else."

SYNERGY

We all know of a Panchtantra story telling us 1+1 = 11. A single person is all alone. He/she can accomplish a little whereas when there are two persons (i.e., one plus one) they develop much greater energy. It was the great achiever Helen Keller who said : "Alone we can do so little, together we can do so much."

There is another Panchtantra story my grandmother used to narrate to us when we were children. A lion was sleeping. A mouse in a playful act, started tickling the nose of the sleeping lion. The irritated lion caught hold of the mouse and was about to pound it with its paw when the mouse appealed for mercy, stating that some day it might come in useful and may be able to help the lion. The lion roared away in laughter and let the mouse go.

But within a month after this incident, the lion got caught in a nylon net. Despite its best efforts, the lion could not get out and started to roar for help. He was surprised to see the mouse with his friends getting on the net and within a short time, the lion was free. This is both an example of networking and synergy in the animal world.

Man has been aware of the progression of energy by united action since the beginning of civilisation simply by observation and experience. What is synergy? How Top Achieving People (TAP) incorporate it in their way of life to achieve their purpose?

WHAT IS SYNERGY?

Synergy, according to the Chambers Twentieth Century Dictionary, is the combined or coordinated action or the increased effect of two substances, as drugs, obtained by using them together. Again synergism is the doctrine that the human will and the divine spirit are two efficient agents that cooperate in regeneration.

Synergy is the act of working together of two or more people or even of two or more tangibles or intangibles to create a better solution than either could alone. "It is not your way or my way but a better way."

This means synergy takes place at the personal or a single person's level between different attributes of a person's personality, skills and competencies as well as between two or more persons.

SYNERGY AT PERSONAL LEVEL

A magnet is an excellent example of the power of synergy. A magnet has all the molecules facing in one direction, whereas a piece of iron has molecules in haphazard manner. A magnet is organised from within which gives it an immense power.

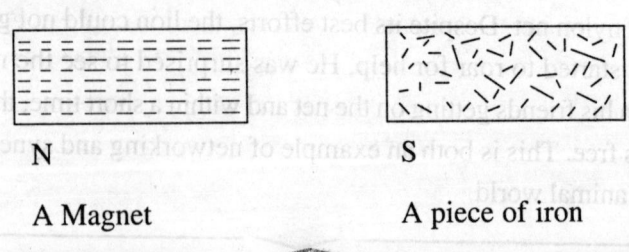

A Magnet   A piece of iron

You can see synergy in the way all the fingers are clasped together into a fist, signifying solidarity, a united and single directional effort. Synergy is a strength that stems from unique people who direct all the positive energies to achieve a unity of purpose in whatever they do. We will be able to understand synergy at the personal level by studying the following diagram :

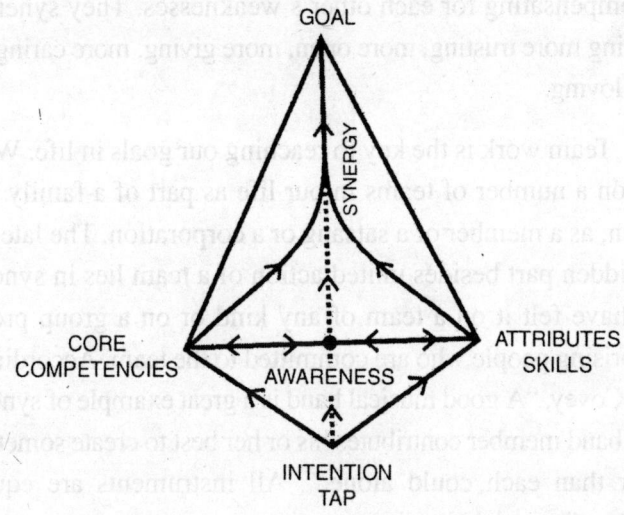

The diagram shows how the three-phase energy generated by (1) your intention plus awareness, (2) attributes and skills, and (3) core competencies go to develop synergy for the final thrust to the goal.

Synergy is the reward Top Achieving People (TAP) experience as they get better at integrating and directing positive attitudes and skills – both interpersonal and interactive-with core competencies and their vision. The synergy so developed propels them to the goal.

Any action in synergy with others is like developing several times the power of the people participating in a task. Synergy is when the whole becomes greater than the sum of its parts.

Top Achieving People synergize with others to accomplish great tasks. They create synergy through cooperation with others – by accepting each other's differences, by respecting those differences, or taking advantage from each other's strengths and by compensating for each other's weaknesses. They synergize by being more trusting, more open, more giving, more caring and more loving.

Team work is the key to reaching our goals in life. We all play on a number of teams in our life as part of a family, as a citizen, as a member of a satsang or a corporation. The latent or the hidden part besides united action of a team lies in synergy. You have felt it on a team of any kind or on a group project comprising people who are committed to the team. According to Sean Covey, "A good musical band is a great example of synergy. Each band member contributes his or her best to create something better than each could alone.... All instruments are equally important".

Synergy is democracy in action, where you find people with different styles, traits and characteristics. The difference is : Are we effectively synergizing ?

Top Achieving People (TAP) realise early in their life that differences among people are a source of strength. They develop a commitment to celebrating these positive differences and find themselves on a winning path.

Synergy is more than just compromise, or cooperation. According to Sean Covey, "Compromise is 1+1 = 1½. Cooperation is 1+1 = 2. Synergy is 1+1 = 3. It is creative cooperation with the emphasis on the word creative. The whole is greater than the sum of its parts".

SYNERGY ACTION PLAN

Discussion among members towards evolving the best approach to tackle a project or an issue in a cooperative and friendly manner forms the focus of a synergy action plan. There will, of course, be differences, opposing view points and approaches but these all get sorted out during brainstorming sessions and help in formulating the best approach or solution which is bound to lead to success in any enterprise.

The wonderful by-product of synchronised teamwork or an action in synergy is that it builds positive relationships that motivate the participants to become Top Achieving People (TAP).

SYNERGY IN AN ORGANISATION

An action in synergy has a four-fold impact on an organisation. It strengthens and improves employees individually by bringing out the best in each one of them. It makes them efficient in their respective fields of work. The employees become self-motivated by deriving satisfaction and taking pride in their synchronised teamwork.

This results in improving both quality and productivity of the organisation and directly leads to the strengthening of the organisation itself.

This aspect of synergy needs greater attention of management gurus for it goes a long way in automatically addressing major HRD concerns like keeping the employees motivated, improving quality, productivity and retention of useful employees.

Don't over organise. Let's not be slaves to Rules and Procedures. Make sensible rules that make for efficiency.

COMMUNICATION SKILLS

In the foregoing, we discussed how Top Achieving People (TAP) develop and build relationships at various levels which create harmony and goodwill and make collective action or teamwork possible in every sphere of life. This builds up their confidence level and they experience synergy to tackle bigger and tougher tasks in life.

Top achievers are aware of the significance and potential of communication skills in building positive relationships. They try to sharpen these skills by observation, training and practice for they realise that communication skills are the cement that binds relationships.

Communication is the lifeline of all human activity. Most of what goes on in any human endeavour is nothing but communication, or something to initiate communication or to keep it going. This is why you need to master the art of communication to make a mark in life.

WHAT IS COMMUNICATION

There are three basic elements in communication. The source or sender, the message or symbol and the destination or receiver. Effective communication requires efficiency on the part of all three. The communication must have adequate information. The communicator must be able to present it in symbols the receiver will understand. He must have a channel that will carry the message to the receiver. The message must be within his/ her capacity to understand. And it must motivate the receiver's self-interest.

To communicate effectively, the sender's words must mean the same thing to the receiver that they do to the sender. The more thing words and fewer nothing words the communicator uses, the easier is his/her message to understand. In short the scenario is something as follows :

1. What the person speaking intends to say
2. What the person speaking actually says
3. What the person speaking is understood to have said
4. What the hearer wants to hear
5. What hearer actually hears.

With all the above possibilities affecting each sentence or a group of sentences, the possibility of misunderstanding is tremendous.

To add to this complexity is the fact that the hearer is also sending verbal and non-verbal messages back to the speaker simultaneously. Whether these can be understood correctly, misunderstood or ignored makes the entire process very complicated.

BARRIERS AND DISTORTION

Barriers to understanding and distortion of message exist in the communicator and the audience alike. Each person lives pretty much by his/her own symbols and stereotypes. There are social barriers, age barriers, language or vocabulary barriers, political and economic barriers. Finally there is the constant noise of competition for people's attention.

Dr. Asha Kaul of the Management Development Institute says a communicator must assure the message being sent out is of interest to the receiver. Any lack of interest on part of the receiver or a message that has not been properly worded leads to what she calls "switching off" the mind. The communication thus should be worded so as not to hurt the sensitivities and feelings of the receiver. The receiver's ego or preconceived ideas act as deterrents to the listening process.

The above analysis hints at our knowing the attitudes, habits, interests and needs of the people we want to communicate with and the language and symbols that have meaning for them.

HOW TO COMMUNICATE

Effective communication means tailor-made message specially designed for the situation, time, place and audience. Cutlip and Center, writing in Effective Public Relations, say the barriers to communication point towards the need for continuity and repetition of a consistent message in simple form and the use of a variety of media that converge on the audience from several avenues.

EFFECTIVE COMMUNICATION

The moment you convey any kind of idea or message, you are communicating. But you are "getting through" to someone only when you learn the words and the "music" which people like to hear.

Top Achieving People (TAP) in every field of life, make positive use of the three basic elements of effective communication to achieve their positive objective and, in the process, also help the people they are communicating with.

This means you have to know people. You have to know what makes them tick. The moment you "begin to pluck the heartstrings of humanity" and help people to make up their mind or formulate a policy on an issue of immediate concern to them, you are a successful communicator. You have motivated them to action.

The people get interested in communication if you tug at their heart strings. How do you do that? According to J.V. Cernon it depends on "how you tie your communication to their every day desire for security, power, skill, affection and love, knowledge or even for mental and physical well-being."

GETTING MILEAGE OUT OF WORDS

The most important tool of communication is words. To get the best result out of words, you have to use short sentences. The mantra is - KEEP IT SHORT AND SIMPLE (KISS).

The following guidelines will be of help :

- Use short sentences, structures and smaller words.
- Use names.
- Use personal references.
- Avoid complicated figures of speech.
- Avoid the abstract.
- Put your finger on the facts and point them out in brief.
- Use words efficiently! Use contrasts! Use comparison.
- Hold their attention – captivate them.

BASIC PERSONAL COMMUNICATION

The following basic guidelines for communication skills can be made a natural part of one's personality. Whatever be the level of one's communication skills, it can be improved with practice and diligence.

LISTEN : STOP TALKING

It cannot just be a chance that God gave us two ears but only one mouth. He did that for a reason. We have earlier discussed the barriers to any communication. In view of these deterrents to the listening process, it is essential for one to concentrate on what is being said.

A mother brought her son to a teacher for coaching him speech and debate. The tutor on interviewing the boy found him to be a chatterbox. He said he would gladly tutor the young boy but would charge twice the amount he normally charged.

The mother naturally asked for the reason since, in her view, the boy already spoke quite well.

The teacher replied., "I must teach him two things instead of one ; first, how to hold his tongue, and then to use it."

The best way to improve the listening process is to improve concentration by regular practice, and judge content and not the delivery. According to a study, we pay attention to verbal content 7 per cent of the time, the voice articulation 38 per cent and the body sport 53 per cent. By reducing attention span on last two components and increasing that of the first, our listening would be more accurate.

BE FRIENDLY - SMILE

You can communicate and get through a person only if he/

she is at ease. Look for signs of nervousness, shyness or other body language signs and try to build relaxation with your smile and friendly disposition.

Focus On What Is Said - Do Not Respond

To encourage the other person to communicate you have to give a positive feedback by your body language and convey that you are interested and want to listen. You have to concentrate on what he says rather than your response. A wrong focus will make you misunderstand the thrust of other person's argument. Formulate your response only after you have listened.

Ask Questions

Get additional information or clarification if required. Ask questions that draw out new relevant facts and ideas to make for better understanding.

Remove Distractions

Try your best to remove distractions and be an enthusiastic listener. Distractions like music or noise disturb the communicator.

Be Patient, Show Respect

Besides being an attentive listener, show respect to the speaker. Benjamin Disraeli said, "Patience is a necessary ingredient of genius". It equally applies to communication.

Empathise - Do Not Criticise

There would be no arguments and wasted time and effort if we learn to see things from the speaker's/communicator's point of view. We should empathise rather than criticise.

When Angry Count Ten

There should be no communication when we are angry. It is better to count ten and calm down before speaking. The attempt to resolve the issue, if any, should be done in a peaceful frame of mind.

Avoid Arguments

Criticising or arguing makes the other person defensive and closed to communication. Approach the issue in a positive and tactful manner. For instance, an employee can be told that he is a good worker and you appreciate his contribution. You would, however, like to correct something that happened during night shift.... This approach begets positive results.

Answer Question And Then Explain

Answering a simple question with long winded explanation makes for poor communication. Go ahead and answer the question directly and follow with a brief explanation.

Precede Unfamiliar Question With Brief Information

Giving a brief information or reference before asking a question helps to draw appropriate and helpful response.

Come To The Point Early

Coming to the crux of the matter early or talking to the point makes for effective communication. It does not keep the listener wondering what you are upto and also prevents him from jumping to the wrong conclusion.

Scope Of Subject Should Be Clear

Having a clear idea of the scope of the subject i.e., how big is the project, what is the budget etc., saves time and makes the listener think within those parameters.

Repeat Important Point For Emphasis

Effective communication requires repetition of what you want to get done or the thrust of your argument. This also lays emphasis on whatever aspect you want to highlight.

Make The Listener Respond

An attempt should be made to draw a verbal response from the listener to make sure you are communicating successfully. This also creates rapport with listeners and generates interest.

Seek Listener's Views

It is quite clear to everyone that arguments cannot overcome any disagreement. An experienced communicator tries to find a solution by listening attentively to the other person. You are fully aware that listening is the answer and not talking. It is during this process you are able to come up with an appropriate response to overcome the resistance and to make the other person agree to your point of view.

HOW TO GET FAVOURABLE RESPONSE

There are times when even a very skilled and experienced communicator has difficulty in getting a favourable response especially when presenting a new idea, new procedure or a different way of handling things. He may be faced with any of the three standard responses : (1) Rejection (2) Partial Acceptance or (3) Acceptance.

Top Achieving People (TAP) try to increase their chances of getting a new idea accepted by using the following guidelines :

MAKE THEM SEE/UNDERSTAND IT

It is futile to try to gain someone's acceptance of a new idea or procedure without first trying to make him understand it. You can expect a positive response only when he understands it. A new procedure in manufacturing has to be demonstrated to get its acceptance.

MAKE THEM BELIEVE IT HELPS PERSONALLY

You have to make the other person genuinely believe that the new idea or process will help. It will be better for the purpose as well as serve his personal interests.

MAKE THEM BELIEVE IT HELPS THE ORGANISATION

While a new idea or process might help someone personally, it will still be objected to on the ground that it will harm the organisation to which a person belongs. Here, the communicator has to be prepared by prior research to convince him how the idea is quite consistent with the purpose of the organisation and explain the benefits to the organisation.

MAKE THEM BELIEVE THEY CAN DO IT

Sometimes a person may not be able to accept the new idea despite the best of your persuasive skills because of some physical handicap or difficulty in understanding the new procedure. In such a situation one should be able to tailor his response by offering encouragement or even training to get the idea accepted.

STEPS TO WIN OVER CUSTOMER

The following guidelines will help in winning over a customer and making a sale :

- Get them thinking positively :

    (a) Make him/her say yes; eliminate all negatives
    (b) Say things that are agreeable to overcome resistance
    (c) keep your sales pitch positive.

- Know what is in the other person's mind; listen to him with full attention. Learn by listening and watching.

- Understand other person's prejudices.

- Watch for preconceived ideas.

- Know how the other person feels. Understand his emotions, prejudices, hurts, hates, suspicions, fears and above all his wants.

- Demonstrate sympathy and understanding.

- Admit when you are wrong.

- Compliment tactfully.

- Get people to make decisions - "A sale is never a sale until it is closed".

People don't like to make decisions. So help make the decision for the customer. Then ask him/her to agree with you. This could be done as follows : "Lets do this .... is that OK? or Let's get together tomorrow at such and such time, OK?" This technique works because : (1) A decision gets made. But the customer does not have to make it. (2) It's common language to say OK without meaning much and actually it does not sound like a closing of the deal. But the customer feels committed to some extent. (3) It gets the job done. The customer has three options. He likes your decision and goes with it (results in a sale); he does not like it and won't go alongwith it (no sale). That gives you a two out of three closing average.

SMALL GROUP COMMUNICATION

Top Achieving People (TAP) in business, industry and social organisations have become increasingly conscious of the importance of keeping in touch with their immediate co-workers, employees, customers, shareholders and the like. Today's managers and chief executives spend more than 60 per cent of their time in group activities, says Kenneth Blanchard.

Any successful communication is directly proportional to your ability to understand and peep into the public mind or the mind of your group. It is dependent on the ease with which you gain access to people and get them to believe what you have to say.

Each person in a group has different personality with strengths and weaknesses. Some minds are open. Some minds are closed. Some are easy to penetrate and others are totally negative and closed to human relationships.

Public Relations gurus have given tips on ways to classify the minds of people. These are :

(1) Great minds discuss ideas; (2) Average minds discuss events; (3) Small minds discuss people.

DEALING WITH PROBLEM PEOPLE

J.V. Cerney in his book "Talk Your Way to Success With People" refers to the minds of people as roadways and classifies them as : (1) The Freeway Mind; (2) The Toll-Round Mind; (3) The Roadblock or Detour mind; and (4) the Dead-End Mind.

Jim Dornan gives a comprehensive classification of common problem personalities based on their negative attitudes. We shall very briefly note against each how to deal with these people based on Jim Dornan's suggestions :

- The helpful type : Inspite of his good intentions, this person can make things difficult. Handle him by "asking him to summarise the discussion" at the end of a meeting.

- The obstinate person : This person resists all ideas and suggestions. Handle him by "asking the group to comment on his behaviour."

- The wet blanket : This person always points out the worst aspects of every idea suggested. Handle him by "asking him to suggest an alternative every time he points out something negative."

- The too amiable person : He/she is an amiable person who agrees to every idea good or bad. You may acknowledge his/her remarks and then ask others for their opinion.

- The arguer : This is an aggressive personality who argues for argument's sake and enjoys it. Handle him by "drawing attention to the objective of the meeting".

- The incoherent type : This person has good ideas but he

has difficulty in expressing his thoughts. Ask him to "repeat his ideas in better language without hurting his feelings".

- The talkative person : A person who repeatedly talks to others during a meeting. Handle him by "calling him by name and asking an easy question. Do not try to embarrass the person."

- The absent minded person : Try to arouse this person's interest by asking a simple question or ask his opinion and compliment him on the response.

- The grumbler : This person is a grumbling type who wastes lot of time and distracts everyone. Handle him by reminding him of the pressure of time. "Ask him to see you after the meeting."

There are many types of people that we come across in various spheres of activity. And most of them will be a combination of the types discussed here. It makes it much easier to work with everyone in the group once you learn to identify and deal positively with problem people.

PREPARE FOR MEETINGS

- Prepare Agenda - It projects a positive image of your professionalism. It enables others to join you in a positive and fruitful discussion.

- Prepare key members individually before the meeting.

- Use visual aids.

- Anticipate possible questions and have the answers ready.

- Enter the meeting with confidence.

- Avoid common hindrances that devalue meetings. This means : (a) Do not hold regular meetings without any topic for discussion; (b) Circulate the topic prior to the meeting so that participants come prepared; (c) Person incharge should know how to conduct the meeting; (d) Do not hold a meeting in emotionally charged atmosphere; (e) Do not drag on the meeting too long.

DEVELOP YOUR PEOPLE'S PERSONALITIES

Top Achieving People (TAP) make a consistent effort to develop the potential of the people for whom they are responsible. This is done in the following ways :

1. Teach Them – Spend time with them on a regular basis. Train and encourage them.

2. Expose them to other good leaders and thinkers. Suggest books, tapes, seminars that will help them learn.

3. Empower them by delegating responsibilities. This will help their growth and increase their abilities.

IMPROVING INTERNAL COMMUNICATIONS

Ignorance of the facts causes gossiping and needless resentment. Some CEOs are unnecessarily secretive. They hold back information as a matter of practice. They tell the employees only the minimum facts needed to handle their jobs. That's a serious mistake. You can't stop people from thinking and wondering.

Mountain Bell once asked people how they thought communications within the organisation could be improved. The responses he got are valid even today. These are :

- Share important information first thing in the morning before people get involved with their work.

- Disseminate information quickly before rumours spread and delink the impact of your message. Keeping people well informed, promptly, is essential to getting their cooperation.

- Emphasise benefits and how these will effect them.

- Give opposing view points on a controversial matter. People can be trusted to think and they would appreciate your confidence in them.

- Don't overload with information. The majority of people find 15-30 minutes at a time most comfortable. If more need to be said, bring it out in a question and answer session.

- Bring in experts to handle subjects you are not comfortable with.

- Ask managers at all levels to help spread the word within the company.

- Follow up communications with reinforcing materials and information. Repetition is the key to retention.

- Make an impressive presentation. Poor presentation is not effective.

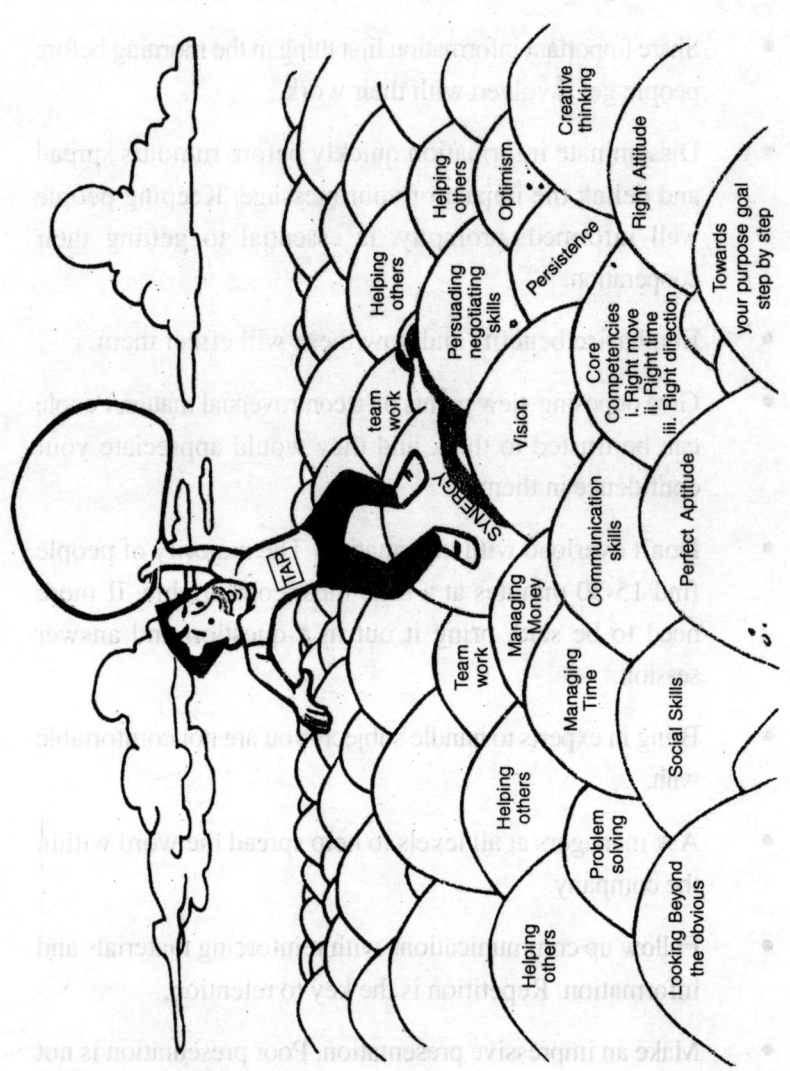

The Path of a "Self Making" man

COMMUNICATION AND SUCCESSFUL JOB SEARCH

THE RESUME

Almost every one of us have to apply for a job one time or the other in our life either to find our first job or to look for better prospects. It is most important to make the CV (curriculum vitae) in the right format. It can make the difference between your getting an interview or not.

FORMAT

Your CV should be no longer than two sides of A4 paper typed in an easy to read font and typed on good quality white paper. It should be error free with adequate space for margins to reflect precise and clear thinking. Exemplary CVs have ample white space to highlight key information and it uses bullets that billboard your accomplishments.

You have to keep in mind that the CV is your advertisement to sell yourself as a marketable person. You have to carry out a bit of personal research on the organization and the job requirements to tailor your CV to suit the needs of the organization you are sending it to. This gives you an edge over other applicants in putting your best foot forward and even in negotiating for salary. But think carefully before embellishing your CV, as recruiters are now increasingly on their guard about misleading claims. Again you have to stress upon your work experience that is most relevant to the job requirement. For this reason it is important to forward your CV with a covering letter.

Your CV should consist of the following sections:
Name
Address
Telephone, e-mail
Marital status
Age and Date of Birth
SUMMARY: Profile and objective

Sell yourself – who you are – why you are writing this CV. Bullet key achievements in a couple of sentences. Avoid long summaries as these can leave the reader with no idea as to when and where your achievements occurred. Use plenty of positive words but don't go overboard.

SKILLS :- Bullet your skills (on the business side)

- Fluency in spoken and written foreign language, if any
- Good marketing skills
- Proficient use of Internet etc.

EDUCATION:- Detail your academic qualifications in the reverse order. Include details of any special courses of study or training in India or abroad. Include your class XII results/education if they are impressive.

EMPLOYMENT HISTORY:- This should also be given in reverse, dated order listing your previous employers and your job description. You need not give your reasons for leaving a particular job at this stage.

PERSONAL INFORMATION

INTERESTS AND HOBBIES:- Include details that buttress your case – say, your ability to work under pressure.

COVERING LETTER:- Your covering letter should specifically state how you are the right person for the job and what you can offer to the prospective employer in terms of your skills and experience. Priorities this list from the point of view of the employer by visualising what is most important to him/her.

Tell him how you can value add to his business. This will show the prospective employer that you understand the environment in which the company operates in.

If possible find out the correct person dealing with the recruitment and send a copy to him/her by fax. You also e-mail it to them with a brief note.

Make your CV flawless and error free. Read it word for word and even ask some one else to read it thoroughly.

YOU CAN GET THE JOB YOU WANT

PREPARING FOR JOB INTERVIEW

If you know yourself, know the company and know about the job profile, you can be almost certain you would be selected in the interview.

Harvey Mackay, the author of the best-seller, "Swim with the Sharks Without Being Eaten Alive," says if you want the job you have to prepare to win it.

KNOW YOURSELF

You should know your interests, your skills and your strengths. You should have clarity about your goals and where do you want to get in future if you get the job you are applying for. This process is quite clear to you from your reading of this book. "Almost anyone can learn to carry off a good interview," says placement consultant Evelyn Davis. "You may not be a sales person, but you have a huge advantage. You know the product – yourself – better than anyone else."

KNOWING THE COMPANY

You should have a thorough knowledge of the company before you go there. Your yard stick of measuring the worthiness of a company has to be unique to yourself. You should chose your employer on the basis of consistent business growth and value based systems. Interaction with the people already working there can be very useful source of quick information. You may visit their web site to acquire knowledge of their product. Harvey Mackay gives a comprehensive list of do's for prospective candidate for an interview as follows - "Did the candidate write a letter beforehand to tell us, the company, about himself/herself, what he/she was doing to prepare for the interview and why he/she would be right for the job? Was he/she planning to follow up the interview with another letter indicating his/her eagerness to join us? Would the letter be in our hands 24 hours ahead of the interview (meeting)".

Now a yes answer to all of the above questions should be quite reassuring to you that you are way ahead on the road to success.

ANTICIPATE QUESTIONS

Management consultants Donald and Diana Stroetzel say any job interview ultimately comes down to eight basic questions and the right answers. We are bulleting the questions here to give you a flavour of what to expect at an interview and to be prepared for it.

- "Who are you really?"
- "Why are you on the job market?"
- "What can you do for us?"
- "What are your strengths?"
- "What are your weaknesses?"
  (Always try to show you profited from your mistakes)
- "What type of boss do you like?"
  (A competent and strong leader I can learn from)
- "What are your most significant achievements?"
- "What salary are you looking for?"
  (If pressed don't quote a low figure nor ask for too much. Be realistic.)
- In your parting words – summarise why you would be right for the job.

BEHAVIOUR-BASED INTERVIEW

This interview is nothing but a conversational interview mixed with a line of questions that elicit your actual behaviour "in a variety of real-life or hypothetical circumstances". Here the emphasis is placed on your accomplishments and abilities than on the basics of your job duties or your opinions.

This interview is best handled by making use of your asset statements. Emphasise here what you can do for the employer in the near future.

REFERENCES FOR THE RECENTLY UNEMPLOYED

Management Pundits say that just because your last job ended badly doesn't mean you are handicapped. With appropriate advance planning and preparation you can limit its effect in your search for a job.

ASK OLD BOSS - You can certainly ask your previous employer/boss if he is willing to give you a good reference. It is very much possible that he would do it. Seldom does a person wish to see you unemployed. You would be able to generate mutual cordiality and enthusiasm in him by telling him how you benefited from his monitoring.

ALTERNATIVE REFERENCES - According to Michael B. Laskoff in case the old boss would not be an appropriate reference you can provide references of other supervisors, out-side consultants and former peers who "had the opportunity to observe your work and can reflect on your skills."

EXPLAIN JOB LOSS POSITIVELY - It is most important that you be prepared to "explain the circumstances of your job loss or a gap in your career in a positive manner". This is much more important than providing references, says Laskoff. He continues, "I strongly recommend that you work out your account in advance and then offer to relate the information proactively in the interview." Finally, remember there is always a good answer to every question. You should anticipate and be prepared for questions about yourself, on your goals and your previous boss and answer these creatively.

KNOW THE JOB PROFILE - If the job profile is such that it focuses on your strengths and offers you scope for further development in the company you should go ahead and accept it even if pay packet is not tempting. You should choose a job that offers you an opportunity to develop your full potential. This will make your chances of reaching your goal faster and easier.

INTERVIEW AND BODY TALK

From the foregoing discussion on how to communicate effectively you are already aware that the way you speak is as important as what you speak. Non-verbal communication speaks volumes. How you carry yourself, while speaking what you do with your hands, whether you make eye contact – all comprise very important elements of our body language. A proper use of our body talk can make us effective and successful communicators. On the other hand distracting movements leave a poor impression and imply that you are nervous, impatient or bored.

The following tips may be kept in mind prior to and during the interview-

- Pick the right clothes. Follow the professional dress code.
- Always smile when you enter.
- A good firm hand shake with eye contact helps them warm up to you.

- Sit forward when you talk and appear animated.
- Do not fidget; pay attention.
- Stay focused. Answer questions in not more than three to five minutes.
- Convey how you are the right candidate who can fulfil the company needs. Build trust. Do not over emphasise your skills.
- Say don't know, if you don't know an answer.
- Discuss pay packet towards the close of interview after you get a hint that they want to hire you.
- Close the interview. Ask for the job at the end of the interview. Clearly state your interest in the company and the position offered.

We have to keep in mind that job interview is not just a passive oneway question and answer session. You don't just sit there passively, politely answering questions. Many talented people don't make it despite their skills just because they do not know how to market themselves. While you are not supposed to brag and blow your horn, you should make a very effective use of your "asset statement" which will make you stand out in the large number of candidates.

While highlighting your key strength areas do mention your transferable skills (like ability to make good business presentations, great at liaising and coordinating etc.) in addition of course to the content knowledge specific to the job applied for.

LEADERSHIP

Top Achieving People (TAP) are keen observers of successful men and women. They are avid readers of biographies of great men. As a matter of fact, each person develops a particular liking for the great personality whose lifetime achievements and the way he/she overcame difficulties and failures appeals to them the most. They try to imbibe these qualities to achieve positive leadership role in their sphere of activity.

Leadership is a quality of working with other people and leading them with a flag towards the achievement of a great victory. Small tasks can be handled by an individual but great tasks cannot be achieved alone.

It has been said that the stature of a leader is determined by the strength of his convictions, the height of his ambitions, the breadth of his vision and the depth of his love.

A leader works with people and shows them a vision. He inspires them to perform at their optimum level with his personal charisma and convictions. He convinces them to believe in him and his ability to lead them to victory.

A leader with authority in business and industry is likely to define and structure his/her role and that of the followers or employees in search of goal attainment. This type of leader expects his/her followers to maintain definite standards of performance and is very particular about meeting deadlines. He always defines roles and tells people what, how and when to achieve it.

The capability of making on the spur decision distinguishes a leader. Such a person thrives on pressure and is able to lead in time of crisis. This kind of leader is very successful in the current environment requiring quick response capability.

Timing is the most important element for a leader. Wise leaders are sensitive to the currents of change and to emerging trends. They do not try to impose fixed ideas on events. They let their minds be open and keep a sense of the movement of things. They see things in the 'round' and are able to judge which way the wind is blowing.

John W. Gardner in his book "On Leadership" says, "The future announces itself from afar. But most people are not listening.... The sound of the new does not fit old perceptual patterns and goes unnoticed by most people.

"And of the few who do perceive something coming, most lack the energy, initiative, courage or will to do anything about it. Leaders who have the wit to perceive and the courage to act will be credited with a gift for prophecy that they do not necessarily have."

Leadership is thus determined by a person's character and vision, his positive beliefs, spirit of sacrifice and the ability to communicate and motivate.

LEADERSHIP DEVELOPMENT

A dynamic leader in any sphere of activity (political, social or economic) is one who is basically an empowering leader. His very style of functioning, vision and charisma make Top Achieving People (TAP) gravitate towards him. Besides imbibing the qualities and sharing his vision, these followers consider the leader as their role model.

The empowering leader has the quality of empowering the people. He identifies, tracks and develops future leaders, top achievers or CEOs among his followers or employees. In a way such empowering leaders serve as catalysts to the development of high performers.

In the socio-political field, Gandhiji was such a leader who attracted the top talent of the country in very large numbers around him. He inspired, moulded and directed them to lead the country during the Independence struggle and take over the reins of the country after Independence.

The names of J.R.D. Tata, G.D. Birla and Dhirubhai Ambani immediately come to mind when we think of empowering business leaders. They have shown high degree of resilience and farsightedness in encouraging and developing intellectual capital.

The idea of developing fast trackers or top achievers for development of future leaders has caught on rapidly with all leading industrial-business corporations. There is a growing realisation here that the future progress would depend on these people. They are continuously engaged in the process of identifying high performance people and training them.

The recent trend towards introduction of "intrapreneurship" has given a further boost to the demand of CEOs at various levels within an organisation. In a way each division head would be CEO and behave like one. In such a scenario, you simply cannot afford to wait for decades to reach the top and then learn how to behave like one. Hence the urgent need for the development programmes that get to work on people at various stages or levels within an industry or an organisation.

According to the American Society of Training and Development every year $50 billion is spent on some kind of executive development programmes or the other.

IDENTIFYING HIGH PERFORMERS (TAP)

High performers or Top Achieving People in a business organisation have been identified to have the following positive traits :

1. They are willing to accept and act upon feedback.
2. They have the ability to reconcile self image and the organisational image.
3. They readily accept external orientation beyond their own line of work.
4. They have the ability to develop core competencies.
5. They show potential and development possibilities.

COMPONENTS OF LEADERSHIP COMPETENCY

The leadership competency consists of the following five components :

- Directing others
- Developing vision.
- Influencing and persuading people.
- Build-up mind set of people for team work.
- On the spur decision making capability.

EFFECTIVE LEADERSHIP STRATEGIES

It has become imperative for the business leadership to revise and review management doctrines and strategies in the new IT environment. The challenges and opportunities arising from the changed environment has equally influenced the attitudes of the people, customers and behaviour of the markets. The following guidelines will provide the winning edge in the changed scenario :

- Effective leadership enters into collaborative partnerships that would help the organisation to hit the top and to maintain leadership status.
- They are adept at leveraging the company's strengths and competencies to the maximum level to surmount any obstacles.
- They are able to evaluate risks and uncertainties in the market place.
- They have the vision to anticipate new technologies.
- They anticipate and lead market changes.
- They integrate innovation by upgrading existing technologies.
- They give better product and service.
- They maximise human and technology asset value to sustain the competitive edge.
- They want their managers to manage. They want action and a winning average – not perfection.
- They build up mind set for team work.

LEADERSHIP STYLES

Generally speaking there are five types of leadership styles based on the dominant characteristic or the way of functioning of the leader. These are :

1. Dominating leader, 2. Negotiating leader, 3. Persuading style leader, 4. Modelling leader and 5. The Empowering leader.

DOMINATING LEADER

This leader is focused on getting things done. The reactions or hardships of the followers do not detract him. He orders and gets things done. He elicits fear and follows a coercive power path.

This style of leadership is most effective during a crisis or war-like situation. Leaders in democratic societies cannot afford to adopt this style during normal times.

A leader has to carry the followers alongwith him through motivation and good public relations and communication skills. Dwight D. Eisenhower, World War II general, used to illustrate leadership quality by putting a piece of string on a table. He said if you pull, the string follows you, and if you push it goes nowhere. A leader, he said, should take into account how the people feel or think and make use of effective communication skills. He should be able to anticipate the people's reaction to a new idea, concept or policy.

THE NEGOTIATING LEADER

Generally most leaders avoid to take on a situation wherein negotiations are required. They believe that the process of negotiations is based on give and take and as such they would not be able to project a victory or a triumph. They consider that negotiations are time consuming and strain one's patience.

In actual practice this is all a matter of one's aptitude or bent of mind. Experienced negotiators thrive on and enjoy the pressure of negotiations. They have a positive approach and know that negotiations involve working together to come to an agreement.

The negotiating leader thrives on his commitment, communication skills and word power to create a win - win situation for every one. He is assertive, direct and to the point.

He is guided by the following philosophy on the negotiating table :

- Don't be disagreeable to disagree.
- Do unto others as you would have them do to you.
- Be true to your convictions.

A negotiating leader does his homework thoroughly. He undertakes adequate study and research and has a complete mastery over the issue. He works out all the alternatives available to him. Alternatives here include ways to analyse, categorise, evaluate, explain and act in the situation. This assures him a winning edge.

The following principles of negotiations are used by a negotiating leader :

- A leader assures a winning situation for everyone.
- He starts negotiations with high expectations.
- Plans ahead the break off point of negotiations.

- Identifies a variety of options to enhance flexibility and chances of success.
- Carefully considers what appears, at first, to be a meaningless offer.
- Puts a time limit on negotiations.

THE PERSUADING LEADER

In a democratic society a leader in political, business or industrial sector does not indulge in steam-rolling others into his way of thinking. If convinced that he knows what is best for the organisation, the leader uses positive communication and PR to persuade others to his way of thinking. Jim Dornan lists six principles of persuasion in his book, "Success Strategies".

- Show them your conviction - "Passion is the outward display of inward conviction."
- Show confidence.
- Know their feelings and beliefs.
- Give them plausible reason "why they should change, how it helps their competency, builds up their creativity and opens up career development."
- Create credibility.

THE MODELLING LEADER

As teenagers or as adults we are all greatly influenced by the positive actions and behaviour of the people we admire. This makes us follow their positive example.

People who join with you by choice are always more committed to you than those who simply follow you out of fancy, an immediate trend or fashion.

The Empowering Leader

We have already discussed the main traits of the empowering leader. This leader enjoys complete rapport with the followers. He always has his fingers on the pulse of the people, understands their needs, wants and aspirations. This leader motivates and convinces the people that they can achieve what they want by following him.

The test of a leader is what power path he follows and how he uses the power – for personal benefits and self-aggrandisement or for helping and bettering the life of the followers.

The empowering leader's objective like Gandhiji is to empower the people by preparing and training them to hold the reins in their own hands. Thus his success becomes the success of the people.

Dr. Blaine Lee, in "The Power Principle" says these leaders (Persuading leader & Empowering leader) follow the "principle-centered power path". They display patience, integrity, consistency, and kindness. They hold people to higher standard and make them feel worthy and eager to cooperate and follow.

Characteristics Of Empowering Leader

The characteristics of the empowering leaders are :

- They have a grand vision which naturally demands the participation of others.
- They have genuine love for the people and know them thoroughly.
- They are aware of their strengths and weaknesses and are thoroughly motivated.
- They develop leadership qualities in others and are willing to share success.

- They are imbued with spirit of service and are committed to their vision.
- They are role models of success and attract dedicated people of conviction around them. These highly motivated followers determine the height of success of the leader.

"No man will make a great leader who wants to do it all himself, or to get all the credit for it" said Andrew Carnegie. And this is the most important fact of life.

LEADERSHIP AND PUBLIC SPEAKING

You have to walk the bridge of communication whether you are getting to one person or many. All leaders have this gift of the gab. They are able to hold the attention of the audience and get the message across through their personal magnetism and speaking skills. Top Achieving People develop this skill through practice and training.

The following guidelines are helpful for public speaking :

- Plan your speech. Know 'who' they are.
- Write your speech. Summarise each point or idea in a single sentence.
- Rehearse your speech. Put the emphasis on right points.
- Spot receptive faces in the audience and watch whether they are registering the emotion you want to generate.
- Make eye contact and lean toward these people as you address them.
- Create change of pace by exercising voice control. Dramatise your point whenever possible.
- Keep your face alive; keep your body alive, use body language to create and maintain interest.

- Be forceful, direct and show enthusiasm.
- Try to address the audience's immediate concerns or problems.
- Watch for signs of boredom. Perk them up.
- Talk their language.
- Give them a message they can use.

How To Make A Point

Prof. Homer Abeggen says : (1) Picturise your point if you would get through to people, (2) Illustrate your point with area charts, cartoon drawings, movie films, slicks, (3) Provide statistics, (4) Use supportive quotes from well known people, (5) Give a few case histories, (6) Use contrast and comparison. Use word pictures so that they can see what you are talking about.

Make Every Word Count

Stimulate the audience to act. And it will act if what you say interests and excites them.

Influence Them With Strong Vocal Action

Use graphic and action-packed words as you move your audience with strong vocal action.

How To Hold An Audience

- Speak spontaneously. Know what you have to say and say it enthusiastically.
- Make it bright and alive using contrast, comparison and projecting simple yet lucid thoughts.
- Deliver the main message that people want to hear.
- Hold their attention by change of pace.

- Touch their emotions.
- Touch their vanity.
- Touch their needs, wants and desires.
- Touch their pride.
- Sum it up and urge them to action.

CULTIVATE YOUR VOICE

The secret of getting through to people in public speaking and to hold their attention lies in the speaker's voice and a lively facial expression. Cultivate your voice and speak in a well modulated, clear and enthusiastic voice that will become your mark of distinction which people will remember.

Speak with passion and above all use words to stimulate the imagination of the people.

Remember to smile when you are speaking and you would have made a lasting impression.

CELEBRATE LIFE

You are master of your own fate and maker of your own destiny. As you think so you become.

I am sure you are already on the path of self discovery – the discovery of the positive powers of your unique mind. You have by now developed the ability to break down performances into small elements that account for internal processes, such as thoughts and feelings as well as external behaviour i.e., actions to make you a better performer in every area of life.

All philosophers and religious thinkers concede that there are different stages leading to higher development. It is not possible to jump from the lowest stage to the highest without preparation, patience and perservance.

The step by step process outlined for the achievement of your goal in life is nothing but a sadhana leading to affirming your reality, of your asserting your fullness – a total self-integration. You become organised from within.

This self–integration is ultimately a by-product of an "inspired mind" which assimilates all your positive energies for fulfilment in life.

WHAT AFTER THE GOAL

Now such an "inspired mind" is at red heat at this stage of the realisation of your "inclusive goal". It cannot be made to halt abruptly in its tracks on your achieving the goal. This is the most crucial stage which calls for planned and systematic approach to find creative outlet for your positive energies. "Right action must you perform keeping clear at once of akarma (inaction) and vikarma (wrong action)", says The Bhagavad Gita.

According to *Desmond Morris the greatest survival trick of our species is "We never stop investigating. We are never satisfied that we know enough to get by. Every question we answer leads on to another question". All progress is the result of an unceasing effort. New horizons open up as we reach our destination.

"The two great laws of life", wrote Charles Gow, "are growth and decay. When things stop growing they begin to die. This is true of men, business, or nations."

@Ross Perot says, "Something in human nature causes us to start slacking off at our moment of greatest accomplishment. As you become successful, you will need a great deal of self-discipline not to lose your sense of balance, humility and commitment."

GOING FOR ALL – INCLUSIVE VISION

On the accomplishment of your personal or inclusive goal you continue your creative effort and involvement to go further ahead for the third level of your vision which is all inclusive.

---

* Desmond Morris is an American author of the bestseller title, The Survival of the Species.
@ Ross Perot is a leading U.S. business tycoon known for his unorthodox approach. He ran for U.S. Presidential election twice as an independent candidate.

You will increasingly realise that the prosperity generated by e-vision, e-business and the IT environment has not filtered down equitably to the less knowledge capital of the country. Your all inclusive vision will include your involvement alongwith other like-minded people in an effort to rectify this imbalance in social and economic development by following in the footsteps of Mother Teresa to "wipe tears from every eye".

Team worker that you are, you could form a team of communicators to rectify the increasing imbalance in information among vast majority of our people in the wake of new information technology environment. You could educate, inform and secure acceptance of the government and business sectors strategies and policies for the economic development of the country.

> *If you are thinking a year ahead, sow seed.*
> *If you are thinking 10 years ahead, educate the people.*
> *By sowing seed, you will harvest once,*
> *By planting a tree, you will harvest tenfold.*
> *By educating the people, you will harvest one hundredfold.*
>
> ...**KUANTZU**

DIS-SATISFACTION

Should we realise that we have not been able to achieve the highest goal despite our sincere effort, it might make us feel depressed. In such a situation we should review the adequacy of the effort put in by us. We should not lose patience since timing is not of our own choice. No great things are achieved suddenly. Slow and steady wins the race.

It is my most firm belief that our heart's sincerest and purest desire is always fulfilled. But in a rare case, if this does not happen likewise we would have to carry out a bit of self-introspection rather than feel depressed.

Almost all transformation, all commencement of a new life begins with self-searching, self examination or introspection. If this is not there, we will never get anywhere.

It is possible our faulty focus on the 'glory' or gratification on reaching the goal has resulted in failure. We are distracted by this excessive fascination as described below:

> *Desires are never quenched*
> *By enjoyment. It rather*
> *inflames them, as clarified*
> *butter does fire*
>
> ...SWAMI CHINMAYANANDA

> *Many persons have a wrong*
> *idea of what constitutes true*
> *happiness. It is not attained*
> *through self-gratification but*
> *through fidelity to a worthy*
> *purpose.*
>
> ...HELEN KELLER

It is evident that our excessive attachment to the accomplishment of the goal with the intention of self-gratification is the major lacuna that makes us miss the goal and feel unhappy. Brian L. Weiss in his book, Many Lives, Many Masters, says "the tendency to excessiveness in thought and action diminishes happiness. Excesses cloud basic values."

Now our sadhana to develop the positive attitude and the perfect aptitude is something akin to the attainment of what

Buddhism describes as "great perfection". This increases our personal growth and makes us into totally self-integrated human beings. This process in itself constitutes an upward path towards our goal. Whether or not we reach this highest state or our highest goal is not important. The journey itself is infinitely rewarding.

NEGATIVE CONDITIONING OF KARMA

No discussion on human growth and development of human consciousness is complete without a brief reference to the relevance of karma. We will quote here opposing views of leading thinkers and leave you to draw your own conclusion :

Commenting on the law of karma, Swami Parthasarthy says :

> "For every action there is a reaction .....
> your personality is the conglomeration of
> desires accumulated through all your deeds
> from this moment backwards, beyond birth to
> your previous life and even further. As long
> as we have even one desire we are still caught in
> the wheel of karma and will take rebirth in
> this world to try to satisfy that desire.
> We will play again in the "three cities" of waking,
> dreaming and deep sleep. The three cities are also
> known as the gross, subtle and causal bodies, which
> refer to the physical (waking), the mental (dreaming)
> and the unmanifested desires (deep sleep)".

Dr. Deepak Chopra the noted thinker and philosopher on

mind-body connectivity writes on the philosophy of karma as follows :

> "There is an unhealthy emphasis on karma in our belief system, bordering on fatalism. It stifles all initiative and leads to resignation to one's lot in life. Karma is a mischievous word. Karma means conditioning – conditioning from past actions and experiences. The goal of all spiritual experiences is to break the conditioning of karma and not explain it away. That is seeking liberation. Karma is defined as conditioned response. Spiritual warriors do not believe in karma."

It is in our power to choose the better or the worse. It is only when we adhere to evil things we come under the domain of destiny. According to the Greek thinker Hermes, "The intelligent substance remains ever in the same state without change, not partaking of the nature of the things which come into being, and therefore destiny has no hold on it".

As a matter of fact our action(s) in the present moment awareness place us beyond the pale of karma. The noted psychologist *Rakesh Chopra speaking at a symposium in New Delhi on the "Dynamics of success" says when we live in present, "we assume that karma and bhagya are merged in one single moment. The present moment becomes all. Thus we can fullfil our individual and organisational responsibilities without feeling stressed, and this ultimately leads to success".

A Few Last Words

Many of the world's great minds have believed that our best energies surface only if we love ourselves and rejoice in our

---

* Psychologist Rakesh Chopra is the current Chairman, Institute of Corporate Management and Century Health Limited.

uniqueness. Those who value themselves achieve great heights of success. A high degree of self-esteem is the basic ingredient for leading a richer, fuller and meaningful life. An achiever realises that there never was anyone like him, there is no one like him and there will never be anyone like him.

> *Every man has the right to feel that*
> *"because of me was the world created"*
>
> ...TALMUD

> *Who can say more than this rich praise,*
> *that you alone are you?*
>
> ...WILLIAM SHAKESPEARE

> *Khudi ko kar buland itna*
> *ke har tadbir se pehle,*
> *khuda bande se khud puchhe,*
> *bata teri raza kya hai.*
>
> ...MOHD. IQBAL

> *This couplet means : raise your self −*
> *esteem to such an extent that before*
> *planning anything for you even God*
> *himself is obliged to ask you*
> *what is your wish.*